The Pentecostal Paradox

The Pentecostal Paradox

G.J. HOCKING

Foreword by Kurt Jurgensmeier

RESOURCE *Publications* • Eugene, Oregon

THE PENTECOSTAL PARADOX

Copyright © 2019 Gregory J. Hocking. All rights reserved. Except for brief quotations in critical publications or reviews, no part of this book may be reproduced in any manner without prior written permission from the publisher. Write: Permissions, Wipf and Stock Publishers, 199 W. 8th Ave., Suite 3, Eugene, OR 97401.

Resource Publications
An Imprint of Wipf and Stock Publishers
199 W. 8th Ave., Suite 3
Eugene, OR 97401

www.wipfandstock.com

PAPERBACK ISBN: 978-1-5326-8306-0
HARDCOVER ISBN: 978-1-5326-8307-7
EBOOK ISBN: 978-1-5326-8308-4

Manufactured in the U.S.A.   04/18/19

Scripture taken from the New King James Version. Copyright (c) 1982 by Thomas Nelson, Inc. Used by permission. All rights reserved.

Contents

Foreword by Kurt Jurgensmeier | vii
Introduction: The Pentecostal Paradox | xiii

1 The Antics of Azusa Street | 1
2 From Gold Rush to God Rush | 18
3 California the Charismatic Cradle | 35
4 When Hysteria Becomes the Criteria | 47
5 Toggling Tongues | 81
6 Back to Pentecost! Or Not? | 95
7 The Mishaps of the Movement | 107
8 Azusa Street and its Antagonists | 119
9 Parham and the Pentecostal Pandemonium | 127
  Conclusion | 137

Bibliography | 139
Index | 153

Foreword

NEW TESTAMENT SCHOLAR D. A. Carson wrote: "In the entire range of contemporary Christian theology and personal experience, few topics are currently more important than those associated with what is now commonly called the charismatic movement."[1] Unfortunately, many in the Church today would deny that. Therefore, let us be reminded of some reasons that understanding Pentecostalism is among the most important topics for the modern Christian.

Simply put, Pentecostalism is claiming that the spirituality of *hundreds of millions* of Christians now and throughout many centuries of Church history is and was rather pathetic and deficient. Pentecostalism is a rebuke to all other Christians that they have missed out on the greatest outpouring of the Holy Spirit's power in all of human history. If Pentecostal beliefs are true, then non-Pentecostal Christians have suffered a great and unnecessary tragedy, and still are.

But what if they are wrong? Then, hundreds of millions of Christians are living in deep deception regarding their spirituality. Hundreds of millions of Christians have illegitimately boasted of spiritual gifts; they do not have, faked that they do, and misrepresented God and his word. If Pentecostal beliefs are wrong, then they are the ones who have suffered a great tragedy, and still are. Therefore, knowing the truth on this matter should be a foremost desire of every Christian.

1. Carson, *Showing the* Spirit, 4.

The Pentecostal Paradox

There is another reason this debate is important. The claims of Pentecostalism cause even the most mature believers to question their own spirituality. The well-known Bible teacher John MacArthur reflects this concern well when he says: "It seems that the Charismatic movement has separated the Christian community into the spiritual 'haves' and 'have-nots.'" He then goes on to freely admit:

> Although I have devoted my life to preaching sound biblical doctrine that centers on the work of the Holy Spirit in every believer's life, I must confess that by the Charismatics' definition, I am among the "have-nots." And I admit to having asked myself, *are all those people who are supposedly having all those amazing experiences for real? Could it be that I'm missing out on what God is doing? Are my Charismatic brothers and sisters reaching a higher level in their walk with Christ?*[2]

If a man of such learning and conviction has been intimidated by Pentecostalism, then what about less informed Christians?

There are several approaches to the Pentecostal debate. I have written extensively on the biblical arguments against it.[3] However, there is also historical evidence against its claims and beliefs. And this is why Greg Hocking's *Pentecostal Paradox* is a great gift to the Church. In my many years of studying this issue, I have found very few historical surveys of the movement. Most of those were written decades ago. Modern surveys are usually from a Pentecostal perspective and intended to promote the movement. Therefore, a modern, non-Pentecostal survey of the movement's history is an important contribution to this vital issue. Thank you, Mr. Hocking.

The *Pentecostal Paradox* will enlighten a new generation of Christians on the questionable roots of the modern Pentecostal movement. Regardless of how popular it is today; the nature of its beginnings is an important aspect of evaluating its true nature today.

2. MacArthur, *Charismatic Chaos*. 21–22 (Italics in original).

3. For a variety of books on the topic see my website at https://trainingtimothys.org/library/advanced-theology.

FOREWORD

There is another impression I hope this book will make on the careful reader. A recognition of the modern Church's arrogant and costly disrespect for how centuries of godly Christians have viewed Pentecostal claims. Such claims have plagued the Church from the beginning. As early as the year 170, the forefathers of Pentecostalism, the Montanists, had to be confronted. There are several remarkable things about them that directly apply to our current topic.

First, their similarities to modern Pentecostalism are undeniable. They claimed a special experience of the Holy Spirit, practiced a version of the gift of tongues that did not involve miraculously speaking in foreign human languages, and they claimed the gift of prophecy, but never accurately predicted the future.

Secondly, the Montanist movement was extremely popular. Church historian Philip Schaff writes: "The frantic movement spread from Rome to North Africa and threw the whole church into commotion."[4] The similarities between second century Montanism and twenty-first century Pentecostalism are remarkable. But there is one convicting difference. The Montanists were almost universally condemned as unbiblical and dangerous to the spiritual health of Christians. Accordingly, Kenneth Latourette, Professor of Church History at Yale relates:

> The first synod [gathering of early Church leaders] was held to deal with Montanism. The movement was condemned as heretical, and its adherents were expelled from the Church and debarred from communion.[5]

The very first false teaching that was popular and serious enough to bring the leadership of the second century Church together was Montanism. It was condemned for the very things that are practiced in Pentecostalism today.

Claims to the miraculous gifts of the Spirit occurred sporadically among Christians until around 1900 when modern Pentecostalism began in America. Without exception, these self-proclaimed

---

4. Schaff, *History of the Christian Church*, II: 110.
5. Latourette, *A History of* Christianity, 129, 132.

"movements of the Spirit" were condemned by the most spiritual, committed, fruitful, and learned Christians of their day. The Jansenists, French Prophets, Shakers, Irvingites, and early Mormons all emphasized precisely what Pentecostalism emphasizes today. And they were all condemned as unbiblical, dangerous, deceitful, and divisive movements of the flesh, if not the devil. I realize that sounds quite harsh, but it is true. Luther, Calvin, Whitefield, Edwards, and Spurgeon all warned their flocks about the dangers of "Pentecostal" beliefs and practices.

Modern Pentecostalism claims that our Christian forefathers were misguided in their reaction to claims to the miraculous gifts of the Spirit. One modern scholar labels such concerns as "bigoted extremes."[6] But it cannot be denied that for the first 1900 years of Christianity, claims to the miraculous gifts were extremely rare, and when they did arise, they were denounced and avoided like a spiritual plague.

Unfortunately, in our day, most will not dare to question or evaluate the biblical nature of Pentecostal claims. Our forefathers had the discernment, biblical knowledge, and courage to protect the Church. The Modern church does not. Which is another reason Mr. Hocking deserves our appreciation. He has provided us with a careful and courageous critique of perhaps the greatest deception to ever infiltrate the Church of God.

And we should not be surprised by all of this. One of the foremost arguments that Pentecostalism makes for its legitimacy is its popularity. But those with more biblical discernment know such a phenomenon is actually a warning to us. Is it possible that Jesus himself predicted the great deception that would occur among Christians through Pentecostalism when He warned:

> Many will say to me in that day, 'Lord, Lord, have we not prophesied in your name, cast out demons in your name, and done many wonders in your name?' And then I will declare to them, 'I never knew you; depart from me, you who practice lawlessness!' (Matthew 7:22–23)[7]

6. Turner, *The Holy Spirit and Spiritual Gifts*, 347.
7. NKJV

Foreword

That word "many" should make Pentecostals shudder. Jesus did not *predict* and *warn* that "many" people, in *general*, will be deceived about their true spiritual state. On the contrary, He predicted and warned that "many" of a particular kind of Church members would be deceived. And he could not have given a better description of the unique practices of Pentecostalism. Jesus Himself warned that "many" of those who practice the things that practically define Pentecostalism will not only be deceiving others, but be greatly deceived themselves.

Yes, indeed, the topic that the author has laboriously researched and written on is vitally important to you. May the *Pentecostal Paradox* help you avoid the deception that has overtaken so "many."

Kurt Jurgensmeier

Introduction
The Pentecostal Paradox

MANY MONTHS AGO, I started writing what I thought would be a short history of Pentecostalism. Little did I know how in-depth such a subject would be. Exploring this movement's history and its later development throughout the past century is a complicated task. For instance, where do you begin when trying to chronicle a phenomenon in which at least one-quarter of the world's population identifies with, including around 49 percent of all Christians in the United States?[1] I have chosen to start writing this history and analysis at the best place for beginning a narrative: right where Pentecostalism had its roots in Topeka, Kansas, in 1901. The preferred launching point, however, in most other versions is the Azusa Street Mission, Los Angeles, 1906. This is where most agree that the movement first entered public recognition.

Ironically, despite this movement being the fastest growing religious phenomena in contemporary history, we still know little about how it progressed to where it is today. Therefore, in this book, I have tried to shed light on some areas of Pentecostalism that is receiving little or no commentary in various other historical analyses of the movement. This lack of coverage is surprising, given the vast amounts of literature recounting the movement's history. However, most of this material tends to come from Pentecostals written for Pentecostals. These "insiders" mostly emerge from

1. Barna Group, "Is American Christianity Turning Charismatic?" lines 20–32.

xiii

The Pentecostal Paradox

various interest groups, often writing under "denominational and national pressures" to maintain pristine teaching that extols the virtues of the movement.[2] This book, therefore, is different in that it will both inform the reader and evaluate the Pentecostal movement from an outside perspective. That said, I write partly from experience, having spent much of my youth within the Pentecostal tradition, allowing me to explore the movement's rise from both a historical and personal perspective.

In this introduction, let me preface my comments by stating that this book is not criticizing Pentecostalism per se. And so, the reader might note that where possible, today's popular Pentecostal personalities are not named. There are, however, no shortage of news media detailing the extravagant lives of some of these colorful characters, indeed, what a vast array of material this source could give! These issues, though I intentionally sidestep to maintain a narrative form that retells the story of the Pentecostal movement. Therefore, the aim of this book is not to merely document the fastest growing religious phenomena in contemporary religious history, it aims, also to describe the foundations and later developments of Pentecostalism in a way that maintains the interest of readers. Every chapter tries to tell the story of Pentecostalism, weighing up the positives and negatives of the movement, while attempting to keep an unbiased perspective.

In summary, this book is a broad narrative that gives fresh insight into the origins, obstacles, and opposition of a movement, which is presently 600 million-plus members strong and still growing. More importantly, the reader will also enjoy firsthand accounts from contemporary eyewitnesses, whose analyses provide crucial insights, particularly into the Pentecostal movement's formative years.

Has this book shed any light on the mysteries of this vast group? What next for Pentecostalism? I have tried to answer these questions in a candid, and yet a concise way, writing the story of the movement while allowing the reader to be the judge.

---

2. See Anderson, *Varieties, Taxonomies, and Definitions*, 15.

1

The Antics of Azusa Street

CALIFORNIA EXPERIENCED THREE MAJOR events at the beginning of the twentieth century. The first was an earthquake that tore through the state of San Francisco on April 18, 1906. *The New York Times* published a report on the aftermath on the following day, outlining the grim details: "A magnitude 7.8 earthquake struck San Francisco shortly after 5 a.m. April 18. An estimated 3,000 people died."[1] The second notable event was a Pentecostal church movement, now numbering over 600 million followers, which burst into the headlines, incredibly, on the same morning as the earthquake (April 18, 1906). The *Los Angeles Daily Times* reported a "Weird Babble of Tongues" as a "New Sect of Fanatics" was "Breaking Loose on Azusa Street."[2]

The third major event was, of course, Hollywood, with all of its glitz and glamor. It launched in 1910 with *In Old California* as its debut silent film.

Which of these three significant events—would you suggest—had the greatest impact on California? To answer this, consider the question posed by the influential *Economist* magazine in 2006, just one century after the birth of the movement. In the

1. *New York Times*, "The San Francisco Earthquake," 13.
2. *Los Angeles Times*, "Weird Babel of Tongues," 1.

1

article, "Pentecostals: Christianity Reborn," the magazine triumphantly declared, "LA's most successful export is not Hollywood, but Pentecostalism." It added that in one short "century after its birth, Pentecostalism is redrawing the religious map."[3] *The Evangelical Dictionary of Theology* agrees, stating that in their view, the Pentecostals are perhaps "the most vigorous and fastest-growing family of Christians in the world."[4] Similarly, a recent *Life Magazine* article listing the one-hundred significant events over the last thousand years featured Pentecostalism and prominently placed it at number sixty-eight on the list.[5]

Conversely, some critics have branded the movement, initially as a matter of "small moment"[6] and "locally, it is of small account, being insignificant both in numbers and influence."[7] Irrespective of these seemingly small beginnings, others have touted the Pentecostal movement as responsible for reshaping the religious landscape of the twenty-first century.[8] From a core membership of just fifty or perhaps sixty people in a former livery stable at 312 Azusa Street, the seeds of this movement are still spreading all around the world.[9] In one short century after its birth, the Pentecostal movement has grown from a mere handful of followers to a global phenomenon. So much so, the adherents of this movement now number in the hundreds of millions, representing at least one-quarter of all Christendom. More precisely, the Pentecostal movement in the last century has grown to over 669 million followers. Further, many believe this group will top one billion followers by 2050.[10] What is the reason for this remarkable growth?

One reason for this burgeoning growth, as this book will detail as part of the worldwide story of Pentecostalism, directly

3. *Economist*, "Pentecostals: Christianity Reborn," 48.
4. See Synan, *Pentecostalism*, 902.
5. Friedman, *The Life Millennium*.
6. Robinson, *Divine Healing*, 23.
7. Bangs, *Phineas F. Bresee*, 230.
8. Cox, *Fire From Heaven*.
9. See Robeck, *The Azusa Street Revival*, 344–50.
10. Johnson et al., "Christianity 2017," 41–52.

resulted from the Charismatic Renewal in the 1960s. At this time, Pentecostal ideas spread into the mainline churches (more on this in chapter 3).

This book aims to give the reader an understanding of how the Pentecostal movement is among the most powerful, fastest growing religious organizations worldwide. While at the same time, showing how this group, along with its antecedent outgrowths of the charismatic and third-wave movements, are also mired in controversy and biblical uncertainty. To conduct this analysis of Pentecostalism, an in-depth look at this phenomenon will feature eyewitness accounts and critiques from respected authorities within the Christian church. While this book is an overview, its purpose is also to assess and analyze the Pentecostal tradition, along with its counterparts in the Charismatic Renewal and the third-wave phenomenon. This then will enable the readers to draw their own conclusions.

Based on the above, it would behoove any inquisitive soul who may have picked up this book to ponder what could have caused this momentous growth.

With that in mind, let us drill down to the details.

The Pentecostals, who are they?

A typical suburban family was sitting around the dinner table one evening. As accustomed, they were reviewing the day's events. During this time, the teenage son explained to his parents how he had made a friend over the past week. As the boy described the situation, the father could sense that something was on his mind. Upon questioning him, the lad blurted out, "Daddy, [my new friend says] he is a Baptist. I told him we were Pentecostal. Now, just what exactly is a Pentecostal, anyway?"[11]

As noted above, the Pentecostal movement is of recent origin. In fact, before the turn of the twentieth century, you would never have heard the term "Pentecostal" affiliated with any other religious group. Therefore, to grasp the beginnings of the movement, one must first hark back to a small Bible school in Topeka, Kansas, run by the instigator of the movement, who will feature later Mr.

11. Archer, "The Gospel Revisited," xvi.

Charles Parham. Let us go back to the year 1901. On this occasion, an 18-year-old young woman named Agnes Ozman was reportedly the first person to receive what is known in Pentecostal circles as the baptism in the Holy Spirit with the sign of speaking in tongues. From this moment, Pentecostalism began. Before long, the resulting outcome resounded around the world, gladly accepted by some. As the Pentecostal Evangel—the official Assemblies of God magazine—asserts, it was more often than not, "rejected by most."[12] It is interesting to note that when historians discuss the origins of the modern Pentecostal movement, the Azusa Street events of 1906 (which will feature shortly) are usually better known. However, at the same time, discussions often touch on the events in Topeka, Kansas, under Charles Parham in 1901. As far as one can tell, the first-known print mention of the Pentecostal movement appeared in the *Topeka Daily Capital* newspaper on January 6, 1901. In this edition, the article headlined the following, "A Queer Faith, Strange Actions of the Apostolic Believers . . . The Believers Speak a Strange language."[13] Similarly, the 1901 edition of the *St Louis Post-Dispatch* reported that a "new sect in Kansas speaks with strange tongues."[14] These reports focused on a small group of students who broke out in unusual languages in the school mentioned above run by Charles Parham. Some years after Pentecostalism crossed the chasm, attracting public notice in 1906. At this time, African-American William Seymour (to be discussed shortly) took center stage with his first appearance in a small church on Azusa Street in downtown Los Angeles. This moment in history led to the spread of Pentecostalism, as we know it today. In fact, if the Pentecostal movement had not made its media debut on the front page of the *Los Angeles Daily Times*, April 18, 1906, the "newest religious sect that started in Los Angeles," may well have escaped our notice. The newspaper reported on the group's strange antics, describing the participants of the movement as "breathing

---

12. Assemblies of God, "Pentecostal Outpouring," 27.
13. Topeka Daily Capital, "A Queer Faith," 2.
14. St Louis Post-Dispatch, "New Sect in Kansas."

strange utterances and mouthing a creed which it would seem no sane mortal could understand."[15]

WHAT ARE THE BELIEFS OF PENTECOSTALISM?

Up to this point, having reviewed the beginnings of the Pentecostal movement, one question naturally arises: what does this movement actually believe?

In short, the birth of modern Pentecostalism is a call to return to an earlier church era when performing miracles was an everyday occurrence. As such, the followers of this movement practice a phenomenon that they claim to have reignited after a 2,000-year absence from the church. Therefore, Pentecostals, in trying to prove the emphasis of these claims, often seek proof text, particularly from the book of Acts in the Bible. This idea led to an assumption that such an experience should become a regular part of everyday Christian life and not just a sort of "curious by-product of religious enthusiasm."[16]

This subject is looked at more closely in chapter 6, titled Back to Pentecost! Or not? This chapter will discuss how the Pentecostal movement has tried to bypass, or at least leap over, 2,000 years of church history, with little or no explanation of the intervening years.

Since its launch, Pentecostalism has evolved into many variations. However, a distinction that is helpful, as most agree, is to divide the movement into three consecutive waves or phases. The launch of the Azusa Street Mission (1906) marked the beginnings of the first wave of the Pentecostal movement, in Los Angeles, California. The second wave began in Van Nuys, California, Sunday, April 3, 1960. At this time, to the surprise of many, Episcopal Church Pastor Dennis J. Bennett announced a covert Pentecostal experience, involving several church members, to his astounded congregation. Significantly, this event marked the beginning of

---

15. Los Angeles Times, "Weird Babel of Tongues," 1.
16. Synan, *The Holiness-Pentecostal Tradition*, 89.

the Charismatic Renewal. The third and final wave of Pentecostalism originated at Fuller Theological Seminary in Pasadena, California, in 1982. On this occasion, two lecturers promoted charismatic concepts in the classroom (more on this in chapter 3). As a result, explains MacArthur, "Pentecostal and Charismatic theology infiltrated [into] evangelicalism and the Independent Church Movement."[17] In effect, these three waves together formed the nucleus of a movement that has mushroomed very quickly—so quickly, in fact, explains Sweeney—that its growth is "nearly impossible to summarize well."[18] Interestingly, these and other emerging Pentecostal developments were all incubated in California, which is the focus of chapter 3, California the Charismatic Cradle.

IS PENTECOSTALISM A CHURCH OR A MOVEMENT?

The Pentecostal movement is something of a "perplexing phenomenon." Having debuted on the world stage as a fringe movement; it initially occupied a minor place on the Christian world stage. Despite these small beginnings, the modern-day movement has become one of, if not the most, swiftly growing religious movements of the twenty-first century.[19] Many have attempted to describe today's version of Pentecostalism. One commentator, Vondey likens the movement to a "global phenomenon, an ecumenical melting pot, a theological puzzle consisting of a multiplicity of voices and positions, and a major factor in the shaping of late modern Christianity."[20] Although Pentecostalism is a part of the broader church, they often prefer to use the term "movement" to describe their function, rather than being designated as a church per se.[21]

---

17. MacArthur, *Strange Fire*, xv.
18. Sweeney, *The American Evangelical Story*, 150.
19. Vondey, *Pentecostalism: A Guide for the Perplexed*, 1.
20. Vondey, *Pentecostalism: A Guide for the Perplexed*, 1.
21. Vondey, *Denomination*, 103.

At the same time, this movement includes various churches representing over 26,000 different denominations, including over 18,000 within the Third Wave movement alone.[22] Therefore, many perceive Pentecostalism as a grouping of "diffuse global movements and not as centralized international organizations."[23]

An excellent example of this is the Assemblies of God (AG), which has grown into one of the largest of all Pentecostal groups. This organization prefers to describe itself as a "fellowship of congregations," shunning terms such as "church" or "denomination" altogether. As a result, the AG movement considers itself as simply seeking to follow God's will.[24] Similarly, earlier Pentecostal pioneers viewed themselves, not as a historical organization, but rather as a part of an end-times restoration movement in world history.[25] Therefore, in a way, the Pentecostals view their movement as the "epicenter of God's activities" in this world, while simultaneously focusing their interest on churches in which they perceive similar manifestations to their own.[26] In a similar vein, Charles Parham (the originator of Pentecostalism), discussed previously, shunned the word "church" altogether, preferring instead "Apostolic Faith Assemblies," for his gatherings.[27] Indeed, even the Azusa Street Mission, as we know it today, originally used as its official title "The Apostolic Faith Mission." Inevitably, the underlying nuance of the term "Apostolic" clearly reflects Pentecostalism's desire to revert to an earlier church epoch.

THE PENTECOSTAL MOVEMENT'S ORIGINS

Various versions about the originator of the story of Pentecostalism and the rise of the movement itself are rife. As will become clearer

22. Barret and Johnson, *World Christian Trends*, 288.
23. See Adogame, *Pentecostal and Charismatic Movement in a Global Perspective*, 500.
24. Jacobson, *Global Gospel*, 35.
25. Jacobson, *Global Gospel*, 35.
26. Creemers, "Theological Dialogue with Classical Pentecostals," 59.
27. Blumhofer, "Restoring the Faith," 54.

later, most Pentecostals disagree with the movement's birthplace as 1901, at Topeka, Kansas, under eccentric—and at times eclectic Charles Parham—the reputed father of Pentecostalism. Instead, they prefer to identify with the events in 1906 at the Azusa Street Mission as the launching point of the movement. The reason for this primarily stems from the sullied character of Charles Parham. I will discuss this further in chapter 9 titled, Parham and the Pentecostal Pandemonium. That chapter will look at some unorthodox and outlandish views that Parham believed and taught. Given he is the founder of Pentecostalism, as MacArthur rightly put it, "contemporary Pentecostals (and by extension, all charismatics) are stuck with Charles Parham as the theological architect of their movement."[28]

However, we will later discuss that Parham although something of a disillusioned character was nevertheless an observant person. Indeed, he perceived certain irregularities in later Pentecostal meetings. This will become clearer in chapter 5, titled Toggling Tongues.

The main actor in this story so far is Charles Parham. He is the originator of the Pentecostal movement, a fact that is historically beyond dispute. There is, however, another person reputed by many as being, if not the originator of Pentecostalism, certainly a pivotal player in its instigation: that person is William Joseph Seymour the acknowledged leader of Pentecostalism. The details of his life before his Pentecostal involvement are largely unknown. However, detailed sketches of his early life influences are the subject of chapter 2, From Gold Rush to God Rush.

While the precise roots of Pentecostalism are a hotly debated topic, most seem to give credit to the eccentric Charles Parham. However, others favor William Seymour. Despite this, there is little doubt that William Seymour is the well-known face of Pentecostalism. After all, he sat at Parham's feet learning to put together what we now know as the modern-day Pentecostal movement.

---

28. MacArthur, *Strange Fire*, 27.

STUDENT SEYMOUR

The year is January 1906. On this occasion, future Pentecostal leader William J. Seymour, an African-American student blinded in one eye from a previous bout of smallpox, sat intently listening outside a classroom. As he sat learning, his tutor Charles Parham would lecture daily on the controversial subject of baptism in the Holy Spirit. As the hours rolled on, Seymour would become enthralled, eagerly taking in the new teachings.

Most accounts of student Seymour have him ignominiously sitting in the hallway because of segregation laws of the day. However, another (and perhaps more reliable) version, penned by Sarah Parham, the wife of Charles, states that Seymour "was given a place in the class and eagerly drank in the truths which were so new to him and food for his hungry soul."[29] Either way, within earshot, this "hungry soul" planned a new version of teaching about baptism in the Holy Spirit. These new ideas soon developed and blended with traditional Christian teaching and landed on an unsuspecting world.

Not long after these events, an invitation arrived for Seymour to travel to Los Angeles. A rather unassuming building on the corner of Ninth and Santa Fe, Los Angeles, played host to Seymour, as he tested the new teaching, he had learned from his mentor Parham. The leader of this church, Julia Hutchins had heard great things about this keen student. With great anticipation, they awaited his imminent arrival. Immediately after going to Los Angeles, Seymour keenly undertook the work. At this point, however, he knew nothing but the baptism in the Holy Spirit (speaking tongues or unlearned languages), which he had not personally experienced at that stage. Unsurprisingly, not long after beginning his meetings on February 22, 1906, he met with opposition. This controversial new teaching was apparently too much for his hosts, and on Sunday, March 4, upon arrival for the next service the very same evening, they padlocked the church doors. Never one to quit, Seymour took his show to another venue only several streets away

---

29. Parham, *The Life of Charles F. Parham*, 137.

to the home of friends at Bonnie Bray Street, April 9, 1906. After this, it was straight to a makeshift site at 312 Azusa Street, on April 14. As the saying goes, "the rest was history."

THE ICONIC STATUS OF AZUSA STREET

After more than a century, most Pentecostals still view the 1906 launch site at Azusa Street with high regard. So much so that the Azusa Street Mission acts not only as the cradle of the movement yet oddly enough, it is for many "the primary icon" for followers of Pentecostalism worldwide.[30] Indeed, this high regard for this launch site has allowed what some term a "myth of origin" to develop. For example, most historical accounts of the movement state that the "spirit fell at Azusa and then flowed in concentric rings, sparking revivals throughout the nation and the world," which has created an apparent foundation myth, which Creech maintains has persisted until the present day.[31]

It is worth stating here that it was not the actual events of the Azusa Street Mission in 1906 that are in question. These events are beyond dispute and historically well documented. Indeed, many eyewitnesses have attested to the occurrences at the Azusa Street Mission, and there are few (if any) contemporary sources, which dispute this account of modern-day Pentecostalism.[32] What is in question, however, is whether the recording of Pentecostal history has presented only one side of the issue (e.g., the Azusa Street Mission of 1906 as being the central point of Pentecostal expansion).[33] As a result, Pentecostal literature often boosts one particular place of origin over another. This inevitably has dictated the written history of the entire movement.

A good example is the so-called "Azusa Stream" model. This idea maintains that the Azusa Street site in Los Angeles is

---

30. Robeck, *The Azusa Street Mission and Revival*, 10.
31. Creech, *Visions of Glory*, 405–24.
32. Owens, *The Azusa Street Revival*, 64.
33. Creech, *Visions of Glory*, 405–24.

THE ANTICS OF AZUSA STREET

the sole epicenter of the movement.[34] For example, most versions of the movement's beginnings emerge from one work in particular: prominent Pentecostal chronicler Frank Bartleman's *How Pentecost Came to Los Angeles*.[35] This book, originally published in 1925, comprises most of the known information on today's Pentecostal movement. Others wrote chronicles of the movement as well. However, most of these histories seem to have been either neglected or disregarded when documenting the origins of the movement. As a case in point, from 1906 to 1909, there were many other versions of the Azusa Street Mission's events written. Yet, according to Pentecostal historian Robeck, far too many of these stories have their basis solely on either uncritical analysis or a "relatively small number of oral or written accounts, many of them highly biased."[36] In fact, some wonder whether Pentecostalism is a uniquely American phenomenon at all. Others paint a more global picture of the Pentecostal movement's origins, citing other global centers concurrent with the Azusa Street Mission's establishment. For example, Jacobson noted, "Pentecostalism seems to have popped up in a number of places at roughly the same time instead of emanating from any single unified center."[37] Although an interesting aside, it is beyond the scope of this book to detail a global picture of Pentecostal expansion. This is especially so given that the primary concern of this section is to question whether the Azusa Street Mission is the single point of origin of the movement. To this end, the rest of this chapter aims to consider whether a "folklore" notion has developed over time, surrounding the rise of the Pentecostal movement at the Azusa Street Mission in 1906—or more directly—whether this type of thinking persists, even to this day.

To illustrate the status placed upon the movement's beginnings, Pentecostal authors Hayford and Moore went as far as to compare the former livery stable of the Azusa Street Mission with

---

34. Creech, *Visions of Glory*, 405–24.
35. Bartleman, *How Pentecost Came to Los Angeles*.
36. Robeck, *Azusa Street: 100 Years Later*, lines 5–15.
37. Jacobson, *Thinking in the Spirit*, 10.

The Pentecostal Paradox

Jesus's stable birthplace. Alarmingly, after stating these observations, the authors candidly added, "and so the story became part of Pentecostal folklore as 312 Azusa Street became an immortalized address in their collective history, becoming the catalytic birthplace of the modern Pentecostal movement."[38] Therefore, the comparison here shows the high regard held for the launching point of the Azusa Street Mission. Accordingly, explained Ziefle, "the central myth of Azusa Street, does seem a bit simplistic in its formulation . . . the attractiveness of having a single starting place was too convenient to ignore."[39] Even so, as it often the case—legends often tend to evolve with retelling—the events of the Azusa Street Mission are no exception. As a result, the origins of Pentecostalism have taken on a legendary quality that continues to act as the founding myths for the movement.[40] Perhaps MacArthur sums this view up best by stating that the Pentecostal movement's beginnings "may sound supernatural and even a bit romantic."[41] However, as we will see in the next section of this book, often these beginnings (most of which, eyewitnesses describe as real events) appear at times shrouded in myth and legend. Therefore, in keeping with the tenure of this book, the author will ask the reader to judge whether the following accounts are factual or, conversely, based solely on fiction. As usual, however, it is best to keep an open mind as to the possibilities of such events happening. As such, we must also measure such claims against church history and of course, the Bible to gain an accurate picture of how New Testament phenomena really should appear.

Indeed, most of the following examples of the myths—perhaps legends would be a better term—come from various accounts of eyewitnesses. These accounts often extol the virtues of the movement without necessarily focusing on some of the more extravagant claims made. Therefore, the primary task is to distinguish between fact and fiction, and tradition and truth in the

---

38. Hayford and Moore, *The Charismatic Century*.
39. Ziefle, *David du Plessis and the Assemblies of God*, 12.
40. Conkin, *American Originals: Homemade Varieties of Christianity*, 293.
41. MacArthur, *Strange Fire*, 21.

THE ANTICS OF AZUSA STREET

origins and development of the Pentecostal movement. The difficulty here is that although there are well-established traditions, these seem based solely upon oral traditions, which are not always correct. Also, mingled in with the oral accounts from eyewitnesses are perhaps a touch of fanciful thinking, as the reader may discern in the following stories.

FIRE CAME DOWN

According to eyewitness accounts of the original Azusa Street events, astonishingly, "fire came down," on April 9, 1906, among the faithful gathered at Bonnie Brae Street (a precursor to Azusa Street).[42] Pentecostal historians likened this to the Bible account in Acts 2:3, which states, "Then there appeared to them divided tongues, as of fire, and one sat upon each of them. And they were all filled with the Holy Spirit and began to speak with other tongues."[43] What is the meaning inferred from this? Well, according to Pentecostal authors Hunter and Robeck, this event symbolized "that God had poured out the Holy Spirit . . . as on the day of Pentecost in the book of Acts."[44]

Further to this, other eyewitness accounts tell us that literal "tongues of fire swirled around the room and above the heads of the band of prayer warriors," during some of their meetings held on April 9, 1906.[45] Similarly, descriptions of other phenomena are even more incredulous, and once again, eyewitnesses testify to the validity of these claims. For example, other accounts reported a glow emanating from the Azusa Street building; supposedly, this was all visible, even from blocks away. Other stories tell of explosion-type sounds rocking the neighborhood, all originating from the small wooden mission on Azusa Street.[46] With such stories

42. See Espinosa, "Ordinary Prophet," 37.
43. NKJV.
44. See Espinosa, "Ordinary Prophet," 37.
45. See Espinosa, "Ordinary Prophet," 37.
46. Owens, *The Azusa Street Revival*, 65.

circulating, it is little wonder that the religious community came out "early and loudly" either for or against such phenomena.[47]

THEY TOLD ME THEIR STORIES

We find a similar record of events chronicled in *They Told Me their Stories*. This book originated from sessions with original participants, conducted by author Tommy Welchel some 60 years after the 1906 Azusa Street events occurred.[40] Obviously, most, if not all, of these Azusa Street Mission veterans, would have been quite young at the time of the original Pentecostal meetings, for they related their stories to Welchel in the 1960s. Even so, memories of the events that took place they claim remain vivid. One eyewitness relied upon by sources to narrate the following story goes, by the name Anderson. At the time, he was a 15-year-old youth. According to this account, an ethereal glow radiated within the building as he took part in the early Pentecostal meetings in 1906.

Further, Anderson explained this was a little "hard to explain because it could only be described, but not understood." The description tells of a "smoke-like substance that would glow as God began moving."[49] As the story goes, it was impossible to pick up or blow it away by a fan. However, you could, we have been told, walk in, sit in, breathe it in, but you couldn't capture or bottle it.[50] Curiously, one young man had tried to fill a bottle with this mysterious substance. Unsurprisingly, he found upon awakening the following morning—you guessed it—the bottle was empty.[51] Our witness, Anderson, further noted that sometimes even Seymour became so fascinated with the supposed "heavy mist that filled the room," amazingly, he would at times "take his feet and kind of play

---

47. Owens, *The Azusa Street Revival*, 65.
48. Morris et al., *They Told Me Their Stories*.
49. Morris et al., *They Told Me Their Stories*, 49–50.
50. Morris et al., *They Told Me Their Stories*, 49–50.
51. Welchel, *True Stories of the Miracles of Azusa Street*, chapter 3.

The Antics of Azusa Street

with the thick cloud."[52] Along with this, apparently, some of the children would play hide and go seek in the heavy mist that filled the room.[53]

Another episode of note involved flames of fire that would engulf the little wooden building on Azusa Street. Although he was young at the time, Anderson attempted to describe the blaze that he claims emanated from the building. He explained that it "looked like flames about fifty feet in the air coming down into and going up out of the roof to meet and merge in the sky over the warehouse."[54] As the story goes, the fire department inevitably attended many times to investigate these mysterious so-called blazes. Another eyewitness confirming the story about these mysterious occurrences was a young woman named Julie Carney. While just 17 years of age when these events occurred, Carney recalled that on occasions, the fire department would inevitably arrive to investigate these blazes.[55] Apparently, this happened many times. Upon arrival, firefighters could not smell any smoke, nor detect evidence of any fire. Carney explained after this happened multiple times, she investigated the flames for herself. The flames, it would seem, were visible from blocks away. Upon querying this phenomenon, the explanation given her was that the flames were supposedly "coming down from heaven into the building, and [the] fire was going up from the building and meeting the fire coming down."[56]

Whether fact or perhaps folklore, tradition tells us that one member of the Azusa Mission, Jenny Moore (whom Seymour married in 1908) was not short on talent. By all accounts, and without prior learning during the early days of the Azusa Street Mission, she suddenly received the ability to play the piano. All this, however, occurred without her having ever taken a lesson.[57] Not only did she play the instrument, but legend also has it she

---

52. Morris et al., *They Told Me Their Stories*, 49–50.
53. Morris et al., *They Told Me Their Stories*, 66.
54. Morris et al., *They Told Me Their Stories*, 50.
55. Morris et al., *They Told Me Their Stories*, 37–38.
56. Morris et al., *They Told Me Their Stories*, 37–38.
57. Alexander, *The Women of Azusa Street*, 156.

began singing and praying in tongues of various languages. In her own words, "I prayed and sang under inspiration, although I had not learned to play."[58]

It would, of course, be wonderful if we could reproduce such occurrences in the present day. However, history provides no pattern of such continuing phenomena, except in the mostly oral tradition handed down from Pentecostal folklore. Although some, but not all, of the examples given above, occurred in biblical days, the question before us is this: did the events that the above eyewitnesses are describing constitute a valid experience, or not? As such, problems arise in the recording of these types of phenomena in that each occurrence seems to contain a similar amount of fiction and fact. While it appears that many of the events as outlined above remain mostly unsubstantiated, it would be beneficial if further research could clarify the validity and credibility of these accounts. This would then aid in establishing the reality of these accounts of the Pentecostal movement's early development.

More often than not, in the recording of episodes about the Pentecostal movement's beginnings, historians seem to gloss over some of the more unsavory elements. This will become clearer later as the book delves into accounts from those who had firsthand knowledge and were eyewitnesses of the original Azusa Street Mission meetings.

In later sections of this book, it will also become clear that early in the Azusa Street Mission's history, specific issues arose such as claims that spiritual hypnotists were active in the meetings. Importantly, these assertions came from none other than Seymour's former mentor, Charles Parham during some of the services conducted by Seymour at the Azusa Street Mission in October 1906. Further, claims such as this came just months after Pentecostalism's beginnings. These concerns, along with other accounts, come under consideration in the formation of a basis that will review the Pentecostal movement in a balanced way. Such a review would be timely, given that specific potentially significant issues are rarely, if ever, addressed in alternative versions of the Azusa Street Mission's

58. Alexander, *The Women of Azusa Street*, 156.

history. This is especially important, given the claim that to some extent at least, the so-called "humble mission on Azusa Street," is the point from where most, if not all, Pentecostals worldwide can trace their lineage, either "directly or indirectly."[59]

In light of the above, the following chapters will discuss the principal concerns of the Pentecostal movement that have arisen since its establishment. In doing so, this book will examine the foundations laid on April 18, 1906, in Los Angeles. "If the foundations are destroyed," asks Psalm 11:3, "what can the righteous do?"[60]

---

59. Synan, *An Eyewitness Remembers the Century of the Holy Spirit*, 24.
60. NKJV.

2

From Gold Rush to God Rush

DURING THE PERIOD LEADING up to the Pentecostal movement's establishment, California experienced significant changes. The most notable of these was the gathering of people from all over the world to California, staking their claims in the 1848–1849 California gold rush.[1]

The second event of significance was the San Francisco earthquake of 1906. This tragic event earned the dubious honor of being California's "greatest urban catastrophe."[2] Further, it remains among the worst natural disasters in "popular memory,"[3] enduring as a "key memory marker in the city's collective unconscious."[4]

The San Francisco earthquake of 1906 would earn another not-so-dubious honor as well that is its connection with the Pentecostal movement's development, given that both events occurred concurrently. In fact, on April 18, 1906, the *Los Angeles Daily Times* issued its first report on the new Pentecostal movement. This article remarkably appeared on the same day as the tragic events of the San Francisco earthquake.

1. Brands, *The Age of Gold*.
2. Zelizer, *About to Die: How News Images Move the Public*, 89.
3. Zelizer, *About to Die: How News Images Move the Public*, 89.
4. Steinberg, *Acts of God*, 26.

FROM GOLD RUSH TO GOD RUSH

As this chapter will outline, both the gold rush and the earthquake marked a turning point, not only in the history of California but also in the Pentecostal movement's development. The one aspect that imbued these two events with significance was that both affected California, and more directly, made way for the burgeoning Pentecostal movement. Later in this chapter, the discussion will focus on how the Pentecostal movement began, including early media reports of the earthquake's devastation and its effect on Pentecostalism. For now, though, the focus will be upon the gold rush and its relation to this movement's beginnings.

THE BEGINNINGS OF THE GOLD RUSH AND THE LAUNCH OF PENTECOSTALISM

Historically, the gold rush had a significant influence on the future destiny of California. Undoubtedly, this event was the single most significant occurrence in the history of the American West during the nineteenth century. Therefore, this event ultimately influenced California's future destiny in many ways.[5]

By way of background, on that eventful day, the gold rush began as James Marshall, and his team worked at Sutter's Mill in Coloma Creek, California. The day of January 24, 1848, started as usual for carpenter Marshall. He was blissfully unaware; however—this day would be like no other—he was about to enter the history books. While in the course of his daily duty, Marshall and his team glimpsed what appeared to be gold, glimmering in the creek below. Suddenly, the surprising realization dawned that they had struck it rich. From that moment, the California gold rush had begun. After this, as the saying goes, "the rest was history."

After the discovery of gold in the year 1848, so the thinking goes, the California gold rush was inevitable. After all, who would not want to travel immediately to California, if all you allegedly needed to do was to "scoop up" the abundant gold that was just

---

5. Holliday, *The World Rushed in*.

awaiting discovery?[6] Not long after the California gold rush began—news of this discovery spread around the world as fast as the times would allow—first, by telegraph, and then by word-of-mouth. In response to this news, people converged on the Golden State from all over the world.

Most would agree that this discovery at Coloma Creek, California, in the middle of the 1800s was the catalyst for the California gold rush. Similarly, a key "trigger" ignited the Pentecostal movement of 1906, after an earthquake shook California to its core. I will look at this aspect in detail later in this chapter.

The gold rush was ultimately an absolute gold mine in the Golden State. Soon after it began, significant changes occurred in the state; so much so, the population tripled to 93, 000 people between 1849 and 1850.[7] Not long after this, around 300,000 gold prospectors, adventurers, merchants, and immigrants from around the globe converged on California.[8] Remarkably, all this would occur within the space of just a few short years. Another direct beneficiary was Los Angeles. Just over one decade after the gold rush began in 1860; the population experienced phenomenal growth. At the time, only 1,610 people were living in the state.[9] Soon, however, things would change. By the 1880s, Los Angeles's population had quadrupled. By 1890, the city's population had quintupled in size.[10] The burgeoning population growth only continued after the gold rush. By the time of the first-recorded Pentecostal meeting at Azusa Street, in April 1906, Los Angeles was a bustling metropolis. So much so, in the same year, the *Los Angeles Herald* triumphantly reported that the population exceeded 230,000 people in that city alone.[11]

---

6. Eifler, *The California Gold Rush: The Stampede That Changed the World*, 7.

7. See Russell, *The Gold Rush*, 367.

8. Walker and Landau, *A Natural History of the Mojave Desert*, 197.

9. Epting, *Victorian Los Angeles*, 32.

10. Logan and Ochshorn, "Los Angeles and Southern California," 30.

11. *Los Angeles Herald*, "Population is Past 230,000."

FROM GOLD RUSH TO GOD RUSH

Curiously, San Francisco, before the gold rush started in 1848, had been a sleepy desert outpost with fewer than 1,000 inhabitants known at that time by the name of Yerba Buena.[12] Soon, however, this changed considerably. By the turn of the twentieth century, San Francisco acting as a gateway to California saw the population balloon to over 340,000 inhabitants.[13]

During this time, with the vast influx of people, the way was being paved for a new religious movement to begin at the Azusa Street Mission in Los Angeles.

Not long after the establishment of Pentecostalism in the previous century, news of the growing movement filtered out. Soon after coming into prominence, it permanently changed the Christian church. This had a profound impact, drawing people in Los Angeles to see for themselves the events occurring in a former livery stable at 312 Azusa Street, Los Angeles.

THE WORLD CONVERGES ON THE AZUSA STREET MISSION

The Pentecostal movement, particularly in its early phases, shared many similarities to the gold rush. This is especially true in that both events were "chaotic and unplanned," as the influx of people into the Golden State continued after the gold rush.[14] The title of J. S. Holliday's book on the California gold rush—*The World Rushed In*—aptly described the events of the Azusa Street Mission in 1906.[15] Later, it will become clear how this mass influx of people joining the new Pentecostal movement occurred during tenuous times in California. As noted above, an earthquake ripped through San Francisco's heartland in 1906 causing untold damage. In the end, however, this resulted in a sudden realization that something was happening in a "tumbled down shack" in Los Angeles, which

---

12. Walker and Landau, *A Natural History of the Mojave Desert*, 197.
13. Zelizer, *About to Die: How News Images Move the Public*, 90.
14. Borlase, *William Seymour: A Biography*, 96.
15. Holliday, *The World Rushed in*.

resulted in a "God rush" to the Azusa Street Mission that same year.[16] It seems that the world did rush in to witness what was happening, as many flocked to the early Pentecostal meetings. Before long, as Eifler's book described it, just like the California gold rush, the Azusa Street Mission phenomenon was *The Stampede that Changed the World*.[17] So too, many flocked to the early Pentecostal meetings. Indeed, they came, first by the hundreds, then by the thousands, traveling they came from all over the United States (US) and Canada, and then from around the world.[18]

DISTINGUISHING FOOL'S GOLD FROM THE REAL THING

The well-known Shakespearean adage "all that glitters is not gold," applies as much to the religious realm today as it did to the California gold prospectors in the middle of the nineteenth century. The discoverer of gold, James Marshall, proved that time-tested truth firsthand. Before the gold rush even began, he tested the gold to decide if it was real. In a way, this also applies to modern-day Christianity. When a message purports to be from God, it needs testing to make sure it does not depart from the accepted Christian teaching. The real test for this is, of course, the gold standard of the Scriptures. By applying this standard, we can decide both what is genuine or spiritually worthless. However, things are not necessarily always that simple, as will become more evident as this chapter unfolds. Often hidden among the real articles can be the subtly camouflaged false glitter of fool's gold. So then, it would be a mistake to accept every spiritual manifestation as the real thing. Indeed, not all that glitters with religious enthusiasm is necessarily gold.[19] For that matter, many things that seem, ostensibly, on the

---

16. *Los Angeles Times*, "Weird Babel of Tongues," 1.

17. Eifler, *The California Gold Rush: The Stampede that Changed the World*, 7.

18. Schmitt, *Floods upon the Dry Ground*, 188.

19. Pyle, *The Truth about Tongues*, 64.

surface at least, as true religious phenomena may be anything but the real thing.

It might be helpful at this point to refer to a book titled *Strange Fire*. In this work, the author John MacArthur likens the beginnings of the Pentecostal movement to the California gold rush in the context of fool's gold. Further, this book explains that during the gold rush, in their quest for that elusive metal, prospectors soon discovered that "not everything that sparkled was worth keeping."[20] The ever-present danger of mistaking the counterfeit shimmer of fool's gold for the real thing has always been an unfortunate reality. Therefore, in the case of uncertainty, the prospector—similar to the Christian of today—would test the samples to discern the genuine from the fake. After all, the prospector's future and fortunes relied on these tests, not only to authenticate these finds [21] but also to "differentiate the glittery lookalike from the genuine commodity."[22] This problem certainly is as true for us in the twenty-first century as it was for gold prospectors in the nineteenth century, as even the most experienced of prospectors found it difficult to distinguish fool's gold from the real commodity. The reason for this is that sometimes the distinction is not always clear. Similar to the fool's gold, the religious counterfeit can often become confused with the genuine article. Indeed, Sproul and Parrish well noted in this regard that, "in every recorded revival in church history, the signs that follow it are mixed. The gold is always mixed with dross. Every revival has its counterfeits; distortions tend to raise questions about the real."[23]

As this chapter has tried to show, many and varied are the opinions about the attractions of the early stages of the Pentecostal movement's beginnings. The question remains whether all the manifestations or phenomenon that occurred among the early Pentecostals were genuine or came directly from God. Accordingly, Pentecostal historian Robeck noted, "not every manifestation

20. MacArthur, *Strange Fire*, 55.
21. MacArthur, *All That Glitters*, 20.
22. MacArthur, *Strange Fire*, 55.
23. Sproul and Parrish, *The Spirit of Revival*, 22.

or phenomenon at the Azusa Street Mission came from the Holy Spirit."[24] Therefore, it would be fair to ask whether all those attracted to the meetings were true seekers. Indeed, many people came to the Azusa Street Mission initially, as inquirers attracted from near and far to the allure of what to all appearances was the genuine article. The church seemed to have arrived at a similar crossroad, being inundated with new teachings, each appearing to "glitter a little more than the last," wrote MacArthur. However, "as was true in the mid-1800s, just because it glitters doesn't mean it's good. Christians need to be equally wary of fool's gold."[25]

NEW HOPE FOR A NEW CENTURY

It is usual that at the start of a new century, people expect that events with sufficient importance will define the tenor of the century to come. For this reason, at the dawning of the twentieth century, many believed that this turn-of-the-century event would usher into the churches what some considered an original type of Christianity. In California, at the start of the twentieth century, a deep-rooted desire for change swept the entire country.[26] Indeed, at this time, the city of Los Angeles found itself at a crossroad, longing for something different, yet few could agree on the shape that change should take. The form this change eventually took, however, (when Pentecostalism emerged onto the scene) surprised many within the churches at the time.

Ultimately, it seems that the Azusa Street Mission served as a significant turning point in Christian world history, despite its being a seemingly unlikely source for such change.[27] However, armed with a message that both attracted and repelled the masses, Pentecostalism offered something that was both unique and unprecedented for the times. Indeed, "the message that attracted

---

24. Robeck, *The Azusa Street Mission and Revival*, 135.
25. MacArthur, *All That Glitters*, 20–21.
26. Sanders, *William Joseph* Seymour, 82.
27. Synan, *An Eyewitness Remembers*, 21.

multitudes to the Azusa Street Mission," explained Synan "was novel and revolutionary. Essentially, the new message proclaimed that modern Christians could receive the Baptism in the Holy Spirit, just as the Apostles did in the day of Pentecost."[28]

Could it be that this aspect of the new and novel did, and continues to today, attract the masses to Pentecostalism, a movement that has grown to over half a billion people in a little over a century? Of course, this is a difficult if not impossible question to answer. After all, there are so many aspects of this movement; it would be an arduous, if not a fruitless task to define all the factors that enabled its growth. One thing is clear: the proponents of the Pentecostal movement thought they could hark back to the very first era of the church's establishment with claims of biblical evidence to prove it. In fact, they believed that it was a modern-day repetition of the original outpouring of the Holy Spirit at Pentecost in the Book of Acts. It is not only this, however, that initially attracted the masses; it was also the message proclaimed by the Pentecostal movement. In a sense, this message has been just as revolutionary as their first leader and theological father of the movement Charles Parham (introduced in chapter 1). Indeed, he enigmatically drew the crowds through his new and novel message. Similarly, the dramatic claim that a New Testament Pentecost experience was happening again at the start of the twentieth century attracted widespread interest. In the end, this would draw many thousands of visitors to California to witness and partake in this new phenomenon for themselves.

As I mentioned at the start of the chapter, at the turn of the twentieth century, California was primed for change. To be sure, with its rapid population growth, much of the state after the gold rush was becoming something of a melting pot. This was especially so in the city of Los Angeles, which at the time represented a wide diversity of cultures and ethnic mixes. The city at this time was becoming a "laboratory for the new and different," much the same to a certain extent as it is today. In a way, this allowed Los Angeles to become a cradle of "the twentieth-century Pentecostal

28. Synan, *An Eyewitness Remembers*, 21.

The Pentecostal Paradox

tradition"²⁹ (see the next chapter). Ethnically, much of California was diverse; therefore, the Pentecostal meetings offered a certain multicultural appeal to the working-class neighborhoods surrounding the Azusa Street site. In a sense, this mirrored the community around that part of Los Angeles. As a result, this became a beacon of equality and hope, which for many the Pentecostal movement also represented.³⁰

Therefore, it could be said that the Azusa Street Mission in Los Angeles epitomized the African-American experience and "sociopolitical dynamics" existing in the city at that time.³¹

CALIFORNIA'S GREAT EARTHQUAKE

Another of the contributing factors to the Azusa Street Mission's growth, initially at least, was the great San Francisco earthquake of 1906. These were dire times for the state of California because the earthquake rocked not only San Francisco; it also riled the nerves of many. Amid this tragedy, the Azusa Street movement was becoming something of a focal point of interest in Los Angeles. In fact, given that the earthquake and the first-recorded reports of the new Pentecostal movement converged in the same day's news, attention focused on the Pentecostal movement at the Azusa Street Mission. Indeed, this initially caused both believers and cynics alike to take notice of these occurrences.³² Therefore, the earthquake had a "domino" effect, causing hundreds of "nervous Los Angelinos" to rush to the new Pentecostal mission, where they joined in igniting the Pentecostal conflagration that still rages in the present day.³³ Remarkably, it seems to have taken a natural disaster on this scale to spark interest in the Azusa Street Mission, explained Chesnut, as the earthquake shook "the religious soul"

---

29. Sanders, *William Joseph Seymour*, 82.
30. Campbell, *Making Black Los Angeles*, 137.
31. Campbell, *Making Black Los Angeles*, 137–138.
32. Robeck, *The Azusa Street Mission*, 6.
33. Chesnut, *Born Again in Brazil*, 26.

of the nation.³⁴ At this time, during the earthquake devastation, some assumed that the event was providential or even apocalyptic. Indeed, new aftershocks were felt, also in Los Angeles itself only a few days after the initial quake. This had the rapid effect of setting many people on edge, leading some to assume that the San Francisco earthquake was some ominous sign. In fact, as will be apparent shortly, this is how some early Pentecostals wanted the general population to think.

One of the leading Pentecostal voices in those very early days of the Azusa Street Mission was Frank Bartleman, who wrote extensively about the effect of this tragic event on the Pentecostal movement. In his own words, he believed the "San Francisco earthquake was surely the voice of God to the people on the Pacific Coast."³⁵ At the same time, however, he noted that because of the palpable terror, the people of Los Angeles and the cities roundabout were on the verge of the breaking point.³⁶ It even seemed "as though they would fly to pieces," Bartleman wrote, "even on the street, almost without provocation."³⁷ As the fears grew prevalent, the author added, "I found the earthquake had opened many hearts."³⁸

DID GOD SEND THE EARTHQUAKE?

Could it be that God sent an earthquake destroying thousands of people's lives, homes, and livelihoods? Undoubtedly not, yet there were those within the early Pentecostal movement who were working hard to convince people otherwise. Let me explain what I mean. Within days of the earthquake, the early Pentecostals distributed tens of thousands of leaflets, trying to convince the populace that

---

34. Chesnut, *Born Again in Brazil*, 25.
35. Bartleman, *Azusa Street*, 50.
36. Bartleman, *Azusa Street*, 50.
37. Bartleman, *Azusa Street*, 50–51.
38. Bartleman, *Azusa Street*, 47–50.

The Pentecostal Paradox

this was some sort of apocalyptic sign.[39] The question on almost everybody's lips at this time was "did God do that?"[40] In trying to answer that question, immediately after the tragedy, the early Pentecostals wrote another pamphlet. This time it had the simple title, "Earthquake." In this tract, Bartleman raised that very matter when he asked, "What does God have to do with earthquakes?"[41] This publication was from the middle of May, just one month after the earthquake devastation, printed and distributed over 125,000 times.[42] In sharp contrast, however, almost every church in the city (except the Pentecostals) was busy trying to calm people's fears. Indeed, they were "working overtime" trying to prove that God had nothing to do with the earthquake.[43] Many had denied the hand of God in this event, and according to Bartleman, his task—along with some early Pentecostals—was to counteract that influence.[44] However, this only heightened fears, which created an air of uncertainty and feelings of helplessness, as many were seeking to find answers. Further, the consensus was that the earthquake caused the Pentecostal movement's eventual success.

Whether intended or not, the synched timing of the earthquake and the launch of Pentecostalism had its desired effect. Inevitably, this would focus the minds of many people on some elements of Pentecostal thought as an end-of-the-world fear gripped California after the tragedy. These events inclined many Pentecostal participants at the Azusa Street Mission to view this as a sign that the end of days was fast approaching. However, this only drove the already present apocalyptic fear and "gave the movement an urgency, that might otherwise not have been present."[45] Many believed that the earthquake was some sort of divine judgment upon humanity. All this, however; they all too

---

39. Melton, *Encyclopedia of Protestantism*, 492.
40. Bartleman, *Azusa Street*, 47–50.
41. Robeck, *The Azusa Street Mission*, 79.
42. Robeck, *The Azusa Street Mission*, 79.
43. Bartleman, *Azusa Street*, 47.
44. Bartleman, *Azusa Street*, 48.
45. Melton, "William Seymour," 2593.

readily concluded were only the beginning of a series of natural disasters, some believed would occur at the end of days. Indeed, this belief was becoming prevalent among the Pentecostals at this time, even going so far as to warn that Los Angeles would next face earthquake devastation.[46] To support this claim, one member of the Azusa Street Mission, Mary Galmond, revealed that the Lord supposedly showed her visions of the San Francisco earthquake the previous year. Apparently, Galmond received a divine warning that Los Angeles, the so-called "New Jerusalem," would be next.[47] Indeed, this was quite a statement. However, given this warning occurred later in 1906, it would have been after the tragic event in San Francisco.

Further to this, history attests to the fact that, despite this claim, Los Angeles never met such a fate.[48] Amid the already tense atmosphere, Seymour himself purportedly taught that the San Francisco earthquake was the beginning of the great tribulation. Naturally, this had an impact, as ultimately it played on people's fears of further earthquake devastation in Los Angeles.[49]

THE EARTHQUAKE WILL NOT COME ON SUNDAY!

Whether intended or not, the official Azusa Street Mission's communication tool, the *Apostolic Faith* magazine, published a rather bizarre disclaimer in its November 1906 edition. Amid the tense environment in Los Angeles at that time, the retraction stated, "in our last issue, there was a prophecy by Sister Mary Golmond of an earthquake coming to Los Angeles. She stated that the Lord had not showed [shown] the time, but that it would not come on Sunday." The retraction bizarrely added that a word had inadvertently been omitted from the article.[50] In-

---

46. See Blumhofer, *Restoration as Revival Revivals*, 145.
47. Davis, *L. A's Pentecostal Earthquake*, 97.
48. Robeck, *The Azusa Street Mission and Revival*, 80.
49. Tennant, *Theology in the Context of World Christianity*, 163.
50. Hyatt, *Fire on the Earth*, 42.

deed, by leaving out that little word "not" the article read that "the earthquake will come on Sunday!" The retraction, however, should have been an apology for the fears the original article created about future earthquake devastation. Sadly, however, this was not forthcoming from the officials at the Azusa Street Mission, which would have only added to the tense environment already prevalent in Los Angeles at the time.

SEYMOUR'S APOCALYPTIC OUTLOOK

As previously noted, apocalyptic fervor, it seems, was a driving force in formulating the newly emerging Pentecostal movement. Another influencing factor was Seymour himself. As pointed out in the previous chapter, Seymour, over time, may have imbibed some influences from his mentor Parham. However, there were other influences, which would come in the formative stages of his life as well.

Shortly after arriving in Cincinnati, Ohio, at the turn of the twentieth century, Seymour became involved with a group called the Evening Light Saints Movement. This group took its name from a verse in Zechariah 14:7, which states, "It shall be one day which is known to the Lord neither day nor night. But at evening time it shall happen that it will be light" [51] They, in essence, considered themselves as living in the twilight time or the last moments of human history. Their beliefs involved extreme views emphasizing the need for Christians to reject denominations in favor of what they considered "the one true Church."[52] Indeed, this led the group to assume that it was similar to the early church that lived in the morning light of gospel times. In fact, they saw themselves as the end-time generation that would witness what they believed would be the end-time evening light fulfillment.[53]

---

51. NKJV.
52. Hollenweger and MacRobert, *The Black Roots*, 50.
53. Sanders, *William Joseph Seymour*, 52.

A further influence upon Seymour was his association with Martin Wells Knapp, a Christian pastor who ascribed to a similar Pentecostal ideology to that of Seymour, authoring a book in 1898, titled, *Lightning Bolts from Pentecostal Skies*.[54] Curiously, though, it is likely that Knapp and Seymour never met given the premature death of Knapp in 1901. It is, however, possible that William Seymour imbibed several of his radical views, especially if oral tradition is correct, which claims that Seymour attended Knapp's Bible school. Some of these views included Knapp's unique understanding of property ownership. Several examples appeared later in his life, especially from the 1900s, that show this. First, the magazine, he owned and operated changed its name from *The Revivalist* to *God's Revivalist*. Next, his Cincinnati Bible School changed its name to God's Bible School. Knapp also believed it was a good idea to deed his property "to God."[55] In an ironic twist, after Knapp's decease, a court ruled that "God" could not own property, and a court battle raged over God's Bible School. It became the subject of a court-appointed trusteeship, having been resolved only as recently as 1970.[56]

Simply put, these influences, along with the teaching imbibed from his mentor Parham, weighed heavily on Seymour, who was already displaying an inclination toward an end-of-the-world belief system.

Sadly, those who imbibe this type of apocalyptic fervor ultimately, when the expected end-time events do not materialize, struggle to face everyday realities of a harsh world. In addition, in formulating these types of views, many become disillusioned when the expected end-time events do not occur.[57]

Another possible reason for the Pentecostal movement's initial attraction was the ever-present underlying nuance that they were the generation living in the climax of history. In the end, however, the Pentecostal movement's claim of being an end-time

---

54. Kostlevy, *Holy Jumpers*, 132.
55. Kostlevy, *The A to Z of the Holiness Movement*, 179.
56. Kostlevy, *The A to Z of the Holiness Movement*, 179.
57. Anderson, *An Introduction to Pentecostalism*, 61.

movement with reinforcing signs and wonders ultimately engendered hope to an oppressed and marginalized people.[58]

Further, as the new Pentecostal movement developed, it merged with another end-of-the-world group, namely the Metropolitan Church Association (MCA), otherwise known as the Holy Jumpers because of their exuberance. The group was awash with problems, and many regarded it as an extreme holiness sect that had its genesis in 1894. Some relatively extreme views they espoused included advocating communal living and abolishing private property.[59] At the height of the Azusa Street events, a leader in the Burning Bush Association, A.G. Garr (who will feature in chapter 5), closed the mission (part of the MCA), bringing it into the white-hot atmosphere of the Azusa Street movement. As a result, this allowed the two to merge; reigniting the Azusa Street Mission's flame after the effects of the earthquake had subsided.[60] The volatile joint mixture of elements ignited "holiness radicalism" within the movement. Kostlevy, who wrote extensively on this issue, deemed it "part of the radical network," (with whom Seymour was associated) noting the stunning resemblance between the two movements (i.e., the Burning Bush Association and Azusa Street Mission).[61]

Another factor attracted the masses: sheer curiosity. After all, "all kinds of people began to come to the meeting . . . many were curious and unbelieving; others were hungry for God."[62] There was also the added attraction of the new and novel. What is more novel than a "rambling old barn [that] was filled and the rafters . . . so low that it was necessary to stick one's nose under the benches to get a breath of air," as described so charmingly by the *Los Angeles Herald*.[63]

58. Anderson, *An Introduction to Pentecostalism*, 61.
59. Kostlevy, *Holy Jumpers*, 110.
60. Kostlevy, *Holy Jumpers*, 133.
61. Kostlevy, *Holy Jumpers*, 133.
62. Bartleman, *Azusa Street*, 46.
63. *Los Angeles Herald*, "How Holy Roller Gets Religion."

Recalling the Azusa Street Mission over the last century, one cannot help but wonder what caused people to flock to meetings in such droves during the movement's early stages? One reason that is perhaps the most obvious even today is the tongues phenomenon. There would have been rumors circulating (as mentioned in chapter 1) of people hearing of such wonders as "tongues of fire" swirling around the heads of Pentecostal participants.[64] It makes sense that with such rumors going around, word would quickly spread around Los Angeles. So much so, thousands of curious onlookers flocked to meetings to observe the events firsthand.

At one point, the *Los Angeles Daily Times* reported that "meetings are held in a tumble-down shack on Azusa Street, and the devotees of the weird doctrine practice the most fanatical rites, preach the wildest theories and work themselves into a state of mad excitement in their peculiar zeal." Furthermore, they also lay claim to having the "gift of tongues, and to be able to understand the babel."[65]

We must recognize; however, the barn-like atmosphere of the Azusa Street meetings (as described in chapter 1) prompted many to compare the meetinghouse on Azusa Street with the stable of Jesus's birth.

Regardless of the Azusa Street Mission's location and dilapidated condition, multitudes of curious onlookers, spectators, and "spiritual vagabonds" from all around the city, and from all lifestyles descended on the old mission.[66]

What initially attracted the crowds? Parham, who visited the Mission in October 1906, just months after its initial launch, observed, "there are many in Los Angeles who sing, pray and talk wonderfully in other tongues . . . and there is a jabbering here that is not tongues at all."[67] This observation is important, for as we venture into chapter 5, titled Toggling Tongues, what influenced Parham to make such a comment will become clearer. There will

---

64. See Espinosa, "Ordinary Prophet," 37.
65. *Los Angeles Times*, "Weird Babel of Tongues," 1.
66. See Espinosa, "Ordinary Prophet," 38.
67. Parham, *The Life of Charles F. Parham*, 169.

be much more that Parham will have to say about the Pentecostal tongues phenomenon. As such, Parham's contribution to speaking in tongues is relevant and pertinent to the movement's history. After all, his contribution to this phenomenon is much more than simply a "curious footnote," since he taught it to his protégé, Seymour.[68]

---

68. Shapiro and Barnard, *Pentecostal Modernism*, 53.

3

California the Charismatic Cradle

CALIFORNIA HAS GIVEN THE world its fair share of charismatic phenomena. As the cradle of the charismatic movement, most, if not all, within the Pentecostal and charismatic tradition worldwide can trace their origin either "directly or indirectly" to California.[1] Also, as alluded to in chapter 1, most Pentecostal movements worldwide can trace their lineage directly to the events of Azusa Street, California in 1906.

In this chapter, the focus will be a review of the many aspects of Pentecostalism, which all have remarkably had their nexus in the Golden State. Therefore, the priority will be to look at the factors that over time have contributed to California's role as the worldwide charismatic cradle of Christianity. So, is California the cradle of the charismatic movement? One Pentecostal advocate affirms as much when discussing Los Angeles states: "this city has been the cradle of revivals"[2] Adding to this sentiment, Margaret Poloma, in *Main Street Mystics*, asked:

> what better setting for P/C [Pentecostal] narrative than southern California? God seemed to be expressing a sense of divine humor in birthing worldwide

1. Synan, *An Eyewitness Remembers*, 24.
2. Poloma, *Main Street Mystics*, 173.

THE PENTECOSTAL PARADOX

Pentecostalism in an area that would soon become the movie capital of the world!³

Not only has California become the movie capital of the world, but as the remainder of this chapter will show, it has also become the world's Charismatic Capital.

As stated in chapter 1, California experienced three significant events at the beginning of the twentieth century. The first event is the San Francisco earthquake of 1906, followed by the Pentecostal movement's establishment and finally, the origins of Hollywood. However, as briefly alluded to in that chapter, from these three significant events, the question arose: which had the greatest impact on California? The *Economist* magazine provided the answer, stating that in its opinion, Pentecostalism had the most significant influence in California at least.⁴

Given the Pentecostal movement's importance within the Californian context, the question at this stage is how California became the cradle of the charismatic movement in the first place? This is not an easy question to answer—at least not until we consider a brief synopsis of the period leading up to and beyond the launch of the Pentecostal movement of 1906. Additionally, this chapter will illustrate that the three waves of Pentecostalism—beginning with the Azusa Street Mission in 1906—all had their nucleus in California.

CALIFORNIA DREAMERS

At the height of the Azusa Street meetings, in September 1906, little-known writer Robert Whitaker (1863–1944) became pastor of Oakland's Baptist Church. Writing a column for the magazine, *Sunset* in 1906, Whitaker asked an intriguing question reflected in the title, "Is California Irreligious?"⁵ In response to this question, Whitaker explained that he knew "California, religiously, pretty

---

3. Poloma, *Main Street Mystics*, 173.
4. *Economist*, "Pentecostals: Christianity Reborn," 48.
5. Whitaker, *Sunset*, 382.

well," and in his opinion, there was "no field for religious effort more appealing and more inspiring than California."[6] Is California irreligious? No, declared Whitaker, for "forth from our city of Saint Francis and our city of the Angels," he declared, would be the point from where there shall go the "songs and prophecies of the world's best faith."[7] Whether Pentecostalism is the world's best faith is open to debate. Indeed, when the author Whitaker wrote this in September 1906, he was not alluding to the Pentecostal movement per se. Instead, he had dreamed of a better hope for his beloved California.

Another person with great dreams for the Golden State was the Reverend Joseph Augustine Benton. During a sermon at California's Congregational Church in 1850, he aptly described the prevailing mood in California at that time. He claimed the influences of the gold rush would be so vast on California that the world's center would change. California, he believed, would become "the land of pilgrimage" and no one explained Benton, "will be thought to have seen the world till he has visited California."[8]

CALIFORNIA ELECTRIFIES THE WORLD

From the period of the gold rush, prosperity was in store for California, even during difficult times. The publicity generated—whether positive or negative—during this time placed California on the map. Historian H. W. Brands perhaps said it best when he stated, "America's golden dream resurfaced and became a prominent part of the American psyche only after Coloma . . . electrified the country and the world."[9]

After the gold rush, the "God Rush" began, as the world rushed into the Azusa Street Mission house in 1906. Indeed, this became a catalyst of the newly formed Pentecostal movement,

---

6. Whitaker, *Sunset*, 384.
7. Whitaker, *Sunset*, 385.
8. Benton, *Pacific School of Religion*, 11.
9. Brands, *The Age of Gold*, 442.

which was only the first wave of Pentecostalism. However, the story of this movement does not end there. Indeed, as the rest of this chapter will explain, California has truly become a cradle, as the host of no fewer than three epochs of Pentecostalism.

A NEW CONSTELLATION OF PENTECOSTALISM

Around the middle of the twentieth century, a new phenomenon occurred, which Bruner described as a "new constellation of Pentecostal people" arriving on the horizon.[10] This new phase of the Pentecostal movement largely lacked the emotional excitement and frenzied style of worship that can often be associated with the movement.[11] Before this new wave appeared, various independent groups developed that involved charismatic faith healers and so forth. However; they generally operated relatively independently from the classic Pentecostal movement. Over time, the term neo-Pentecostalism gradually assumed the name of the Charismatic Renewal. Eventually, though, this would give to the movement, such credence that it gradually became something of an "inclusive trend within the mainline churches."[12] However, this progression also allowed what was before considered an unacceptable phenomenon to make "subtle inroads" into the staunch mainline churches.[13]

THE THIRD FORCE IN CHRISTENDOM

Indeed, the "New Pentecost" was alive and well heading into the mid-twentieth century. In 1958, *Life Magazine* described a burgeoning Pentecostal movement entering the scene. The magazine referred to this new movement in terms of a "gospel singing, doomsday preaching sect." From this time, the new Pentecostal

---

10. Bruner, *A Theology of the Holy Spirit*, 52.
11. Bruner, *A Theology of the Holy Spirit*, 52.
12. Swincer, *Tongues Volume 1*, 60.
13. Swincer, *Tongues Volume 1*, 60.

movement became known as "an emerging world religion," gaining such prominence that it has now established its place as the "Third Force in Christendom." So dynamic is this Third Force that it is only just a shade numerically behind the other two significant forces of Christianity namely Catholicism and Protestantism.[14]

In certain respects, this new wave of neo-Pentecostalism began, over time, to permeate older institutional churches. This, indeed, was only a prelude to what became the second wave of Pentecostalism, or the Charismatic Renewal, which is the focus of the next part of this chapter.

This renewal broke out during the turbulent 1960s. At this time, the US became embroiled in the Cold War with Russia, while enduring significant conflict in Vietnam. Indeed, much of the US during this time was experiencing unprecedented civil unrest. The Kennedy era was beginning, and words such as "charismatic" were becoming commonplace in describing this vivacious leader. In contrast, at the same time, many of the charismatic persuasion were becoming excited about what they described as a new wave of the Holy Spirit being "let loose in the land."[15] With spirituality at such a low ebb, perhaps this emergence of the Charismatic Renewal was inevitable. Despite the anxieties that existed during the 1960s, many within the broader church wondered about the likely impact of this renewal on their churches as they stood on the outside looking in.

THE BEGINNINGS OF THE RENEWAL

As most would agree, the Charismatic Renewal first burst forth from St Mark's Episcopal Church on Sunday, April 3, 1960. This experience opened the floodgates of controversy, which in turn spearheaded an unassuming middle-class church in Van Nuys, California, into the orbit of charismatic phenomena. It all happened on one pre-Easter Sunday morning, April 3, 1960, after

---

14. Van Dusan, *Third Force in Christendom*, 113.
15. Moore, "Discerning the Times," 282.

presiding minister Dennis Bennett casually strode up to the podium and announced to the assembled congregation about his own charismatic experience of miracles, tongues, and other such phenomena. Along with Bennett, others within the church also testified to having shared similar experiences. The resulting outcome from that defining moment in history is that Pentecostalism crossed the chasm, entering mainstream churches. Since that time, the Charismatic Renewal has spread to practically every "historic church," denomination in the Christian world.[16] Initially, this new wave of charismatic phenomena assumed the name neo-Pentecostalism. However, a diligent Lutheran minister named Harry Bredesen balked at this title for the movement. He penned a letter to the editor of *Eternity Magazine*, stating a preference for the emerging movement to be termed, "the Charismatic Renewal in the historic churches."[17] At the same time, he also coined the phrase "charismatic," which has since stuck, defining a new day for Pentecostalism. At this point, this event would have had little effect beyond Los Angeles had a parishioner not contacted both *Newsweek* and *Time* magazine. *Newsweek* published the headline titled A Rector and a Rumpus. The article stated that although:

> it is considered quite proper today for members of revivalistic and Pentecostal groups to be moved on occasion to praise God aloud in languages that often sound like gibberish and are entirely unfamiliar even to speakers. But when such fervent worship moves members of a suburban Protestant Church Episcopal parish to speak similarly, it can be strange and quite troublesome indeed.[18]

The Los Angeles Daily Times soon picked up the story and ran the caption: "Reverend Got Tongue-Lashing for Beliefs." This article told of an "uproar [that] ensued in the parish over Bennett's disclosure that Episcopalians were succumbing to perceived gifts of the Holy Spirit."[19] Indeed, the besieged rector Bennett an-

16. See Williams, "Charismatic Movement," 220.
17. See Choi, *Healing*, 1068.
18. *Newsweek*, "Rector and a Rumpus," 77.
19. Dart, *Reverend Got Tongue Lashing*, lines 5–8.

nounced his resignation that very Sunday morning, while one of his assistant ministers threw off his vestments in protest, resigning instantly. "I was being tried on the spot," Bennett later wrote when recalling these events.[20]

THE RENEWAL LOSES STEAM

Initially, the Charismatic Renewal undoubtedly gained pace. However, after several years of euphoric existence, this new and exciting wave of Pentecostalism began a slow but steady decline. It seems that as this renewal turned the corner into the 1970s; it slid downhill, culminating and ultimately peaking, as it turns out, after a convention in Kansas City, Missouri. The convention—the Conference of Charismatic Renewal in the Christian Churches— convened in 1977. It drew an unprecedented crowd of over 50,000 charismatic Christians from all over the world.[21] This wave of enthusiasm, though, was short-lived and before long, this newest phase of Pentecostalism appeared to lose momentum before it ever took off. While the Charismatic Renewal affected vast swathes of denominations, practically all mainline churches in the US lost members not long after it even began.

For example, from 1965, just six years after the launch of the movement, it dwindled in numbers.[22] Initially, insiders were hopeful things could turn around through such a renewal. However, the expected turnaround did not occur, and by the end of the twentieth century, most, if not all, of the mainline denominations had lost members in unprecedented numbers.[23] Despite this dramatic decline, nobody knew how to slow the exodus given that by this time, most of these churches lost from one-third to one-fifth of their members.[24] Ironically, it seems that the mainline churches

---

20. Dart, *Reverend Got Tongue Lashing*, line 17.
21. Wagner, *The Changing Church*, 42.
22. Wagner, *The Changing Church*, 45.
23. Le Beau, *History of Religion in America*, ch 7.
24. See Harrell, et al., *In the Sixties and Seventies*, 1073.

The Pentecostal Paradox

where the renewal began ended up in a worse condition than when it started. For example, before the Charismatic Renewal emerged in the 1950s, the rates of growth within the mainline churches outstripped the population growth rates. However, coming into this so-called renewal, the downhill spiral only continued. So much so, we find by the end of the twentieth century; most mainline denominational churches had already lost many of the members gained by the renewal.[25] While it is difficult to define the precise cause of the Charismatic Renewal's decline, it is becoming increasingly clear that the liberal stance of these traditional mainline churches certainly contributed to the loss of so many adherents during this time.[26]

WHAT CAUSED THE DECLINE OF CHARISMATIC RENEWAL?

The charismatic movement is defined in various ways. One description terms it as a "revitalizing movement within established churches, seeking to integrate Spirit baptism and gifts into the organization and practices of mainline churches."[27] However, another and perhaps a more apt analysis (from Jurgensmeier) is that the prominent feature of the Charismatic Renewal was that it had its "beginnings and spread in essentially spiritually dead mainline denominational churches."[28] Further, this so-called "renewal" did not necessarily begin with good teaching or "the preaching of the gospel in these relatively dead churches."[29]

So, why when beginning with such momentum, would a movement so quickly lose its steam and decline into oblivion? This question is important, and the answer seems to depend upon whether the gospel truly unified this new phase of Pentecostal

---

25. See Harrell, et al., In the Sixties and Seventies, 1073.
26. See Harrell, et al., In the Sixties and Seventies, 1073.
27. See Yamane, *Charisma*, 81.
28. Jurgensmeier, *Book 10 God's Miracles*, 347.
29. Jurgensmeier, *Book 10 God's Miracles*, 347.

CALIFORNIA THE CHARISMATIC CRADLE

renewal or ecstatic experiences. Indeed, it seems the central unifying feature of the charismatic movement "is not the truth of the gospel, but rather ecstatic spiritual experiences and physical phenomena like speaking in tongues."[30] Another theory for the slow demise of the Charismatic Renewal, particularly as it headed into the 1990s, was that it was becoming too "diffuse and pervasive."[31]

It is difficult to distinguish what this renewal accomplished in terms of real church growth throughout its tenure. As mentioned before, the impact on the church in hindsight was negligible. The reality is clear, however, even with a casual glance that during this time, charismatic mainline churches lost members in unprecedented numbers. Therefore, it would be of the utmost importance to question the movement's unifying qualities given its lackluster results. There are different sentiments about the achievements of this renewal. One idea is that the charismatic movement is something of a "worldwide phenomenon affecting millions of believers from an extraordinary range of Christian churches and streams."[32] However, such a description would not be as relevant today when alluding to the results of this aspect of the Pentecostal movement.

A good question to ask at this point is whether the Charismatic Renewal ended before it even took off? The contributing editor of *Charisma* magazine wrote a book based on an article in the magazine mentioned above in 2010, implying as much. This book made a startling assertion, which in effect claimed, "the charismatic movement as we know it has ended."[33] Surprisingly, the article noted the need for Christians to leave "behind the excesses, extremes and flaky doctrines that give charismatics a bad name." However, in a more enthusiastic tone, the same article celebrated a "new generation" church that has arisen, which, curiously, "no one has coined a term for this movement yet." The author confidently concluded, at least, "it is growing—and it represents the future of

30. MacArthur, *Strange Fire*, 48.
31. Hayford and Moore, *Charismatic Century*, chapter 6.
32. See Hocken, *Charismatic Movement*, 519.
33. Grady, *The Holy Spirit Is Not for Sale*, 26.

charismatic Christianity."[34] This new generational type of church will feature toward the close of this section, and in the next chapter.

THE FLUID STATE OF THE CHARISMATIC MOVEMENT

Such is the impact of charismatic-type Christianity in 2008; the Barna Research Group pondered whether the US is turning charismatic reflected in the title Is American Christianity Turning Charismatic? The article stated that although only 8 percent of the US population are evangelical Christians, of these, half (or around 49 percent) identify with either the Pentecostal or charismatic tradition. The research also found that one in four—or about 23 percent—of adults, attending protestant churches in the US belongs to either a charismatic or a Pentecostal church.[35] Comparatively, just one decade ago, only three in every ten (or 30 percent) of adults in the US were of the charismatic or Pentecostal persuasion. Today, according to the Barna group that "corresponds to approximately 80 million adults" of the US population who are "filled with the Holy Spirit," believing that "the charismatic gifts, such as tongues and healing, are still valid and active today."[36] On a less positive note, as incredible as these statistics may seem on the surface, if we dig a little deeper, it is soon discovered that 36 percent of those considered charismatic Christians in North America identify with Roman Catholicism.[37]

The terms Pentecostal and Charismatic are incredibly fluid; trying to differentiate between them is, at best, ambiguous. The primary reason for this is that these various self-styled groups go under a plethora of titles fitting into many broad categories,

---

34. Grady, *The Holy Spirit Is Not for Sale*, 26–27.

35. Barna Group, "Is American Christianity Turning Charismatic?" lines 20–32.

36. Barna Group, "Is American Christianity Turning Charismatic?" lines 18–19.

37. Barna Group, "Is American Christianity Turning Charismatic?" lines 55–56.

although they do have one commonality—a shared set of belief systems of charismatic experiences. There is, therefore, very little that distinguishes them from one another; for this reason, as a movement, it is difficult to define. Something most would agree upon, however, is that Pentecostalism has developed in three very distinct waves or phases. Having so far examined the first of these two waves, the focus of the rest of this chapter, and the next will be another aspect of Pentecostalism—the Third Wave movement, which erupted in the 1990s.

HOW DID THE THIRD WAVE MOVEMENT DEVELOP?

It was around 1980, explained Pugh, when "the Charismatic Renewal had died down; Neo-Charismatic networks too had reached a natural summit . . . people were looking for something new."[38] The movement that eventually emerged is now known as the Third Wave of Pentecostalism. This term originated in a telephone interview between C. Peter Wagner and the editor of *Pastoral Renewal* magazine in 1983. After describing "what was going on in [some classes at] Fuller," Wagner explained, "the editor asked me what the name of the movement was. I believe the Lord prompted me." Wagner suggested calling "it the Third Wave, and the term stuck."[39] The classes to which Wagner referred began when he was a church growth professor at Fuller. At this time, he brought John Wimber (who features in the next chapter), onto the campus to supervise and teach these classes, aptly named "Signs, Wonders, and Church Growth." It became an important part of the curriculum at Fuller Theological Seminary, launching in 1982 amid much fanfare. It eventually became the most popular course on record at the College.[40] In these classes, third-wave principles became a part of the curriculum, with a major emphasis on how charismatic

---

38. Pugh, *Bold Faith*, 111.
39. Wagner, *Wrestling with Alligators*, 134.
40. Hummel, *Fire in the Fireplace*, 208.

concepts could be conducive to church growth. A unique feature of this teaching was that it not only analyzed signs and wonders in modern-day Christian churches, it also included practical sessions where students learned aspects of Pentecostal practices in impromptu after-class healing sessions.[41] Fuller, however, eventually canceled this class in 1986 because of the displeasure of faculty, staff, who objected to the charismatic component of the teaching.[42] Even so, this event marked a turning point for Pentecostals, launching the so-called Third Wave movement. This has given way to other emerging Pentecostal movements, which have developed over the last few decades. One of these groups goes by the name of the "mystical miracle movement," which forms part of the New Apostolic Reformation developed by Wagner as mentioned above. This burgeoning new group has been well-defined by Hinn and Wood in their book, *Defining Deception*.[43]

Indeed, space prevents the full exploration of all outgrowths of Pentecostalism in this book. There are many other aspects of the Pentecostal movement not covered in this work, such as the Independent Network Charismatic (INC) Christianity group of churches. This term, coined initially by Christerson and Flory, represents the splinter groups comprising primarily of megachurches, most of which emerged from within Pentecostalism heading into the twenty-first century.[44]

41. Marsden, *Reforming Fundamentalism*, 292.
42. Wagner, *Wrestling with Alligators*, 147.
43. Hinn and Wood, Defining Deception.
44. Christerson and Flory, *The Rise of Network*.

4

When Hysteria Becomes the Criteria

IN THE EARLY PART of the twentieth century, a new religious phenomenon appeared based on the book of Acts in the Bible. Indeed, Luke (the writer of Acts) could not have expected such a movement. Had he been able to foresee this new Pentecostal movement states Packer, "I guess Luke would have been both startled and distressed . . . how some of his latter-day readers would misconstrue him in these matters."[1] The "matters" here referred to is how the book of Acts has influenced Pentecostal thought and teaching over the last century—in particular—how the Pentecostal movement has placed great emphasis upon demonstrative religious phenomena. Historically, this movement accepts charismatic-type experiences (miracles, tongues, etc.) as a normative experience for all Christians. However, as asserted by Packer "clearly, much that cannot be read out of the book of Acts has to be read into it to make the Pentecostal case."[2]

In the preceding chapters, the theme has been how the Pentecostal movement has desired to hark back to an earlier New Testament era over the last century. Additionally, it has been stated how miracles and other such phenomena are, in our day,

1. Packer, *Keep in Step with the Spirit*, 165.
2. Packer, *Keep in Step with the Spirit*, 166.

considered not only possible but also normal in the eyes of modern-day Pentecostals. However, some have raised valid concerns about whether this is not only desirable but if it is even achievable. A good illustration of this is a situation that arose in the life of a Pentecostal minister who published in 1974, a book titled *The Corinthian Catastrophe*.[3] The author, Gardiner, mentioned that before writing the book, he was of the Pentecostal persuasion. He noted, however, that something happened that prompted second thoughts about the movement, which he had come to respect and honor. Evidently, it all began with "nagging questions about the gulf between charismatic practices and scriptural statements."[4] Indeed, these so-called "nagging questions" drove him to study the book of Acts afresh. During this study, he found that "the actions and experiences of the early churches were far removed from the actions and 'experiences' of the modern movement." In some ways, they were as he put it, "completely opposite!"[5]

Given the belief that exists widely within Pentecostal/charismatic circles that supernatural phenomena are a normal part of every Christian's journey, breaking through this wall is at best difficult. This is especially so given that there is sometimes a gulf, indeed a vast gulf between Pentecostal practice and Bible statements.[6] It would seem that much of Pentecostalism, and by extension, the charismatic and third-wave movements, tend to have as their goal what Poloma calls, "fresh experiences of the Holy Spirit rather than doctrine."[7] Following along these lines, a Pentecostal/charismatic leader, the late Chuck Smith observed:

> One of the greatest weaknesses of the Charismatic movement is its lack of sound biblical teaching. There seems to be an undue preoccupation with experience, which often is placed above the word. As a consequence, charismatics

---

3. Gardiner, *The Corinthian Catastrophe*.
4. Gardiner, *The Corinthian Catastrophe*, 8.
5. Gardiner, *The Corinthian Catastrophe*, 8.
6. Gardiner, *The Corinthian Catastrophe*, 8.
7. Poloma and Green, *The Assemblies of God*, 3.

have become a fertile field for strange and unscriptural doctrines proliferating through their ranks.[8]

Despite the above statements, which may sound critical or harsh, the reader should note; first, many Pentecostals regularly read and highly value the Bible. Second, and more importantly, most within the Pentecostal tradition continue to hold to the inerrancy of biblical values as an essential aspect of their Christian faith and practice. Therefore, it should be realized from the outset that not all within the Pentecostal tradition partake of some of the more unusual phenomena presented in the following sections. Finally, many of the Pentecostal/charismatic tradition truly seek to fulfill the scriptural admonition of Colossians 1:10 to "walk worthy of the Lord, fully pleasing . . . and increasing in the knowledge of God." [9] Having said that, in the following sections of this chapter, I would like to shift the focus to various aspects of Pentecostalism, particularly some unusual phenomena associated primarily with the Third Wave Movement. A broad distinction of this emerging proponent of Pentecostalism is the emphasis placed on the restoration of miracles. For this reason; it is often called the signs and wonders movement.

Another distinction of this group, unlike its classic Pentecostal counterparts, is that mostly, third-wave Pentecostals tend to downplay the tongues phenomena as a necessary accompaniment of Spirit baptism. In a sense, this reflects what Poloma termed the "casual Californian style" from which it arose.[10]

THE GROWTH OF THE THIRD WAVE MOVEMENT

Without a doubt, since its launch in the 1980s, the third-wave phenomenon is the fastest growing segment of Christianity. Additionally, this aspect of the movement is by far the largest to emerge from within the Pentecostal ranks. It also has seen the

8. Smith, *Charisma vs. Charismania*, 128.
9. NKJV.
10. Poloma, *Main Street Mystics*, 17.

most significant increase in membership numbers of all Pentecostal groups. In actuality, the total number of this group equates to more than the first two Pentecostal waves combined,[11] totaling 18,810 different denominations with over 295 million adherents.[12] In contrast, the second wave of Pentecostalism (the Charismatic Renewal) comprises some 6,530 denominations in over 235 countries, with 175 million followers in the twenty-first century.[13]

Interestingly, however, by comparison, the original or classic Pentecostals number just 65 million adherents in 740 denominations.[14] Will this trend continue? The short answer has to be yes, given the above statistics (the most recent) came out in 2001. Since then, Pentecostalism has added over 150 million members to their numbers.

Without a doubt, the third-wave brand of Christianity may well be experiencing phenomenal growth, yet without an understanding of this aspect of Pentecostalism's roots, it is difficult to assess its real impact on the Christian church. Therefore, to understand how Pentecostalism evolved into the form it took during the 1980s and 1990s, one must first consider where and how these types of phenomena occurred. Indeed, no history of the Third Wave Movement would be complete without reference to its nucleus, "the Vineyard movement." The background of this movement is that before its leader, the late John Wimber (who featured in the previous chapter) taught third-wave ideas at Fuller Seminary, he launched a church in Yorba Linda, California (part of the Calvary Chapel group of churches) in the late 1970s. Although it was initially a traditional sort of church, it was not long before charismatic and third-wave teaching entered this church under Wimber's tenure.[15] Due to the ongoing phenomena, the Calvary Chapel organization, with whom they had an affiliation, asked them to consider a spiritual split. Curiously, on an even

11. See Johnson "The Demographics of Revival," 59.
12. Barret and Johnson, *World Christian Trends*, 284.
13. Barret and Johnson, *World Christian Trends*, 284.
14. Barret and Johnson, *World Christian Trends*, 284.
15. Smith, *Theologies of the 21st Century*, 214.

WHEN HYSTERIA BECOMES THE CRITERIA

more surprising note, Wimber, himself later split with a Vineyard-associated church in Toronto, which hosted the Toronto Blessing, for precisely the same reasons. The suggestion was that it should join with another movement that shared similar Pentecostal-type phenomena. Therefore, later in the 1980s, Calvary Chapel Yorba Linda not only had a name change, but it also created an entirely new movement.

THE LAUNCH OF THE VINEYARD GROUP OF CHURCHES

Launching from small beginnings, the Vineyard organization—in its initial stages—comprised only a few churches. However, it was not long before Wimber took over the reins of the entire group of churches, and under his tenure, the movement experienced rapid growth. So much so that by 1991, the Association of Vineyard Churches grew to over 550 churches and then by 2011, that number rose to 1,500 worldwide after Wimber passed away in 1997.[16] The Vineyard story is in some respects similar to the launch of the Charismatic Renewal, which featured in the previous chapter. Not only did they both have their beginnings in California—the charismatic cradle—they both had one person who spearheaded new phenomena throughout the church. In the case of the Charismatic Renewal, it was Dennis Bennett. And, as most agree, John Wimber launched the third wave of Pentecostalism. However, the story does not end there. Indeed, the following section of this chapter will focus on what occurred at a Toronto-based church associated with the Vineyard Movement. This aspect of Pentecostalism will feature in some detail as the section progresses, where the question asked is whether what occurred at this Toronto-based church—the Toronto Blessing—really was a blessing. The focus will then shift to two other movements, which saw equally strange manifestations, namely the Brownsville, Pensacola, AG, in 1995, and the Lakeland, Florida AG Church in 2008. The last section of the chapter will

16. Anderson, *To the Ends of the Earth*, 217.

THE PENTECOSTAL PARADOX

focus on the so-called "prosperity gospel" teaching and the related name-it-and-claim-it aspect of the message that still forms a significant part of the modern-day Pentecostal movement.

THIRD-WAVE PHENOMENA

It is important to note that much of the publicity (and by extension, much of the growth) surrounding various areas of Pentecostalism, particularly the Third Wave Movement, have primarily focused on hysteria. Given the widespread concern, within the Christian church and much of the media, this requires in-depth analysis to determine the extent and appeal of this movement within the broader Pentecostal community. An example of the mixed feelings about third-wave phenomena first appeared, as far as one could tell, in the well-known magazine *Christianity Today* in 1994. The magazine published an article with the provoking title Is Laughing for the Lord Holy?[17] The report detailed the phenomenon that appeared mostly among third-wave churches heading into the 1990s. The question pondered was whether this type of phenomenon—marked by excessive laughter "has—prompted Christian leaders and scholars to question whether it is a genuine movement of God or merely controversial hysteria that should be forgotten."[18] Indeed, so prevalent is this type of phenomena; it has even caught the secular media's attention. Most of who have noted the shift in Christian churches from what Hanegraaff has called "the age of exposition to an age of experience."[19] An example of this shift is clear in a national television special broadcast by a major network, titled "In the Name of God."[20] This documentary featured on *ABC* news on March 16, 1995. During the mid-to the late 1990s, the media was abuzz with strange Pentecostal-type phenomena happening mostly within the Third Wave Movement. The *ABC* program

17. Maxwell, "Is Laughing for the Lord Holy?" lines 7–10.
18. Maxwell, "Is Laughing for the Lord Holy?" lines 7–10.
19. Hanegraaff, *Counterfeit Revival*, 10.
20. Goodman, "Television Review," B4.

aimed to report primarily on the hysteria, which occurred within various churches around the US. In the process, the question posed to these churches was whether in attempting to attract "sell-out crowds," they are actually selling out the gospel?[21]

The *ABC* filmed live and broadcast worldwide the events at a Vineyard church in Anaheim, California. Admittedly, while the report was fair, it also noted that these types of churches had become, "the fastest-growing trend in Christianity," which the report stated, promised an emotional encounter with God. Here, seekers apparently can find "miracle healing, self-support groups, and rock music. They can also indulge in or watch weekly 'signs and wonders,' often manifested as shaking, screaming, fainting and falling into trances."[22] Meanwhile, while all this was occurring, the founder of this church, John Wimber, although not willing to endorse all that was happening, thought it best to leave the outcomes with God. After all, he reasoned, people are getting their needs met![23]

Indeed, many and varied are the opinions, especially within Christian media about the third-wave of Pentecostalism, as will be evident in the next section where the focus will shift to an offshoot of the Vineyard movement that occurred in a Toronto church in 1994.

THE TORONTO BLESSING! OR NOT?

An article relating to the Toronto Blessing featured in the magazine *Christianity Today* titled The Enduring Revival.[24] While appearing favorable to the phenomena, the magazine also conceded that it was a "mixed blessing." Indeed, the report (written in 2014) maintained that the "Toronto Blessing in 1994 was odd

---

21. Goodman, "Television Review," B4.
22. Goodman, "Television Review," B4.
23. Goodman, "Television Review," B4.
24. Dueck, "The Enduring Revival," line 1.

and controversial—but its benefits have lasted."[25] However, the question remains whether what occurred in this Toronto-based church was a genuine movement of God or merely controversial hysteria that is best-forgotten. In a similar vein, another Christian media organization suggested that the events at the former Vineyard church in Toronto were the "greatest thing that's happened in the church in the last 100 years."[26] Given the diverse views on this type of Christianity, a review of this phase of Pentecostalism would be timely. Therefore, the first section of this chapter will aim to explore some of the more controversial aspects of the Third Wave Movement, beginning with the Toronto Blessing.

During the early part of 1994, a new phenomenon entered the scene that had its beginnings in a nondescript church tucked behind Pearson International Airport in Toronto. Because of the out-of-the-way location of the Toronto Airport Vineyard Church (TAV), one commentator quipped that it was "somewhere about as likely to have housed a global phenomenon as the average rabbit hutch."[27] Soon, though, the Toronto Blessing would capture much of the Christian world's attention and the media as well. After a while, however, the phenomenon faced criticism from none other than its own organization, namely the Association of Vineyard Churches. In the end, this resulted in a split from its parent church; a name change occurred later in 1995. Since then, the church became known as the Toronto Airport Christian Fellowship (TACF), or, until more recently, in 2009, Catch the Fire Toronto.

THE SPIRITUAL SPLIT

Due to issues of ongoing phenomena, the falling out with this Toronto-based church became severe. So much so that in late December 1995, the international director of the Vineyard movement, John Wimber, personally intervened by flying to Toronto.

---

25. Dueck, "The Enduring Revival," lines 25–55.
26. Strand, "Toronto Blessing," lines 1–3.
27. Govan, *The Incredible Rise of Mumford & Sons*, 18–25.

As a result, the Vineyard movement eventually severed ties with the church. A well-known magazine carried the headline, Vineyard Severs Ties with Toronto Blessing Church,[28] while the *Los Angeles Daily Times* described a Spiritual Split after reporting the Toronto-based church had actually gone "over the edge," by allowing its members to "bark like dogs, swoon to the floor and laugh uncontrollably during the services."[29]

In sharp contrast to this, the AG movement gave their approval in 1995, to the Brownsville Assemblies of God, which would display phenomena similar to the events of the Toronto Blessing. Again, in 2008, this would occur—in another church belonging to the AG—only this time in Lakeland, Florida.[30]

Significantly, one reason for the severing of ties with the TAV involved bizarre phenomena described as "exotic and non-biblical manifestations."[31] In a warning from Vineyard headquarters, the directive to the Toronto Vineyard Church was "to curb or at least not focus on the phenomenon," which had by now become a regular part of the meetings held in this church.[32] The Toronto Church further received warning that the events were not acceptable and, in effect, violated biblical values. In reality, they considered it as being exploitation of those involved in some of these more bizarre manifestations being encouraged to go onstage and speak of their experience in front of the whole church.[33]

TORONTO'S TOP TOURIST ATTRACTION

Despite the falling out with its parent church, the Vineyard movement, the impact of the Toronto Blessing never waned. So much so that the church became one of Toronto's top tourist attractions

28. Beverley, "Vineyard Severs Ties," lines 5–7.
29. Stammer, "A Spiritual Split," lines 5–7.
30. Stammer, "A Spiritual Split," lines 5–7.
31. Synan, *The Holiness-Pentecostal Tradition*, 276.
32. Waxman, "Filled with the HO-HO-Holy Spirit," lines 32–40.
33. Waxman, "Filled with the HO-HO-Holy Spirit," lines 32–40.

The Pentecostal Paradox

with *Toronto Life* naming the church Toronto's number one tourist attraction in 1994![34] As a result, it was not long before the hordes of visitors flocked to this Toronto-based church. In all, over 50,000 unique visitors made the pilgrimage within the first six months of the so-called "blessing" in 1994.[35] By December of that same year, this number rose to 75,000 visitors, with a cumulative total of well over 200,000 who darkened the doorstep of the small church located near Pearson International Airport, Toronto.[36] What was the attraction? Laughter, falling, shaking, roaring like Lions, and of course, people becoming so inebriated (what they call being drunk in the spirit) that they could hardly stand, talk or walk.[37]

THE BEGINNING OF THE BRITISH PHENOMENA

Upon arrival on British shores, the media immediately dubbed it "the Toronto Blessing" referring to its place of origin. Following its debut in that country, flights from London to Toronto often sold out days in advance because of the hordes of visitors traveling to this small Toronto church. At one point, London's *Sunday Telegraph* (1994) blazed with the following headline, "British Airways Flight 092 Took Off from Toronto Airport . . . just as the Holy Spirit Was Landing on a Small Building 100 Yards from the End of the Runway" of the Toronto Airport. From this time, the third-wave phenomenon was no longer unique to the US. Before long, the euphoria spread to over 5,000 churches in the United Kingdom (UK).[38]

Surprisingly, the new wave of Pentecostal phenomena first appeared in an Anglican Church in May 1994. The origins of the British derivative of the Toronto Blessing are interesting, to say the least. It all began with the wife of a pastor from a South West

---

34. *Toronto Life Magazine*, "The Best and Worst."
35. Dueck, "The Enduring Revival."
36. Dager, *Holy Laughter*, 2.
37. Dueck, "The Enduring Revival."
38. Arnott, *The Father's Blessing*, 218.

When Hysteria Becomes the Criteria

London Vineyard Church who had heard rumors of what some called a "tremendous party going on" at the Toronto Vineyard Church.[39] After several euphoric days in the spring of 1994 of so-called "carpet time" at the Toronto-based church, the pastor's wife returned home to Britain, and it was not long after this before meetings similar to the Toronto Blessing occurred in London's Holy Trinity Church in Brompton. From here, the phenomenon quickly spread around the UK.

We now visit the room in the Brompton Church where eyewitnesses reported the following phenomena taking place. Let us picture the scene for a moment where these meetings occurred. According to reports, the meeting was a sort of "a cross between a jungle and a farmyard."[40] One eyewitness claimed that apparently, people were roaring like lions. In addition, there were, of course—bulls bellowing—donkeys and many bird songs. In fact, "every animal you could conceivably imagine, you could hear."[41] It was totally unlike anything that ever appeared in a British church before, as many of the Pentecostal participants joined in with the jungle chorus.[42] All the while, the curate of the Holy Trinity Church sat in a meeting in an adjacent building, oblivious to the chaos that was ensuing.

Meanwhile, wrote Govan, the church's secretary called, disrupting the meeting to state incredulously to the curate that practically your "entire staff are lying incapacitated on the floor." "Is it good?" retorted the curate somewhat inquisitively. "I think so," was the cautious reply. "So," the curate inquired, "what are you doing up?" In a resolute tone, the secretary responded, "I crawled on my hands and knees. It was as if a lightning storm had hit the building," wrote Govan when trying to describe the events, "electrifying everyone ... before throwing them to the floor."[43]

---

39. Govan, *The Incredible Rise of Mumford & Sons*, 18–25.
40. Govan, *The Incredible Rise of Mumford & Sons*, 18–25.
41. Govan, *The Incredible Rise of Mumford & Sons*, 18–25.
42. Govan, *The Incredible Rise of Mumford & Sons*, 18–25.
43. Govan, *The Incredible Rise of Mumford & Sons*, 18–25.

According to one report, as the phenomenon made its way to the UK, the many visitors who made this pilgrimage (despite the extra-biblical occurrences) became convinced that it had been a time of refreshing. This was especially so, after experiencing the "lean years" of the Charismatic Renewal during the 1960s and 1970s.[44]

HAS THE BLESSING BLOWN OUT?

A good question at this point may be whether the Toronto Blessing and other associated phenomena has subsided or is there more to come? Insightfully, on this issue, Walker viewed occurrences such as the Toronto Blessing as the "logical outcome of recent Charismatic developments."[45] Wistfully, he quipped that just as "Pentecostalism rushed into the twentieth century like a hurricane at Azusa Street, Los Angeles, in 1906, perhaps it finally blew itself out at Toronto Airport in 1994."[46] Blow itself out it did! The Toronto manifestation, maintained Hunt, disappeared as fast as "yesterday's news."[47] Those occurrences are now, rarely, if ever, discussed within the Pentecostal and charismatic circles. Perhaps, this makes it less of a fad, and more of an end of the charismatic movement, as we know it, at least in its "Western variant" stated Hunt.[48] Similar to its counterpart, the Charismatic Renewal (see chapter 3); eventually, the Toronto Blessing, lost its freshness, becoming "routinized and ritualized," while in the end becoming little more than a "charismatic tourist attraction."[49] As in the US, so too in Britain, when the manifestations wavered, participants responded in various ways. Some, for instance, sought even greater esoteric phenomena or gave up the church altogether, at least

---

44. See Poloma," Toronto Blessing,"1149–1152.
45. Walker, *Thoroughly Modern*, 70.
46. Walker, *Thoroughly Modern*, 71.
47. See Hunt, *The Toronto Blessing*, 247.
48. See Hunt, *The Toronto Blessing*, 247..
49. See Hunt, *Forty Years*, 209.

initially.⁵⁰ It would seem that many of those looking into the abyss of the Charismatic movement, have abandoned these affiliations entirely.⁵¹

Without a doubt, there is much more to Christianity than exciting experiences and moving from one fad to another. One author, Chan, stated that the Pentecostal tradition is experiencing what he termed "spiritual fatigue" because of the continual search for something new. These seekers feel the "routinization of charisma," and are searching desperately for new experiences.⁵² In a direct response to their search for new experiences, many tend to gravitate to places where the action is happening, continued Chan, "such as Toronto, Pensacola, [which will feature soon] and a host of independent charismatic churches?"⁵³ It seems that many are turning to alternative Christian spheres of action in their desperate search for something more. However, all that such "spheres of action" offers are exciting experiences, and eventually, the novelty of these intermittent experiences tends to wear off. So, has the Toronto Blessing and other such phenomena finally worn off? Walker explained, "the momentum of the movement is passing. The craze, like modernity, seems to be fading with a final gasp."⁵⁴ Eventually, like all fads, the phenomena are short-lived, and the momentum wanes. In reality, these ecstatic-type experiences begin to blow out eventually, and once the laughter, frivolity and other antics disappear, the so-called "Blessing" begins to lose its freshness. As a result, some churches where these types of events occurred would return to business as usual while others, having experienced this type of phenomenon crave something more.⁵⁵

50. See Hunt, *Forty Years*, 209.
51. See Walker, *Thoroughly Modern*, 70.
52. Chan, *Pentecostal Theology*, 8.
53. Chan, *Pentecostal Theology*, 8.
54. See Walker, *Thoroughly Modern*, 70.
55. Poloma, *Main Street Mystics*, 215.

The Pentecostal Paradox

DISPLAYING OR DISPLACING THE GOSPEL?

One concern with the third wave's emphasis on miracles and such like is that according to Smith, as the esoteric and ecstatic phenomena increases, this eventually leads to "displacing the traditional preaching of salvation" in churches.[56]

In fact, according to Armstrong, within the Third Wave movement, "anecdotes abound in which unbelievers came to faith without any communication of the person and work of Christ" at all.[57] An excellent illustration of this relates to a situation that occurred during the height of the Toronto Blessing. The leader of this church, while being initially puzzled about what was happening in the church, thought that it might be a good idea to view it as a party instead. He mused, "I didn't know that God believed in parties, but it turns out that he throws the best party in the whole universe!"[58] Sadly, this so-called "party" did not evidently involve preaching Bible-based messages. Not for want of trying, though, because paradoxically, as the senior pastor of this church discovered, fewer people actually responded when the party music was dim, and he preached salvation messages. As a result, this toning down of the gospel inevitably led members of this Toronto-based church to lament the lack of results, and at times, church members would say, "that's not a revival, a revival is when hundreds of people get saved, and the community is impacted."[59]

For his part, therefore, the minister did what all good pastors did: he resumed preaching the gospel. However, in doing so, he felt the meeting had lost something—the ministry time was as he put it—difficult. The next step, of course, was to pray, asking God why it had become so hard.[60] The narrative continues, with the pastor confessing that the response surprised him. "It is because you are pushing me," was the reply. "Lord, I do not want to push you. What

---

56. Smith, *Theologies of the 21st Century*, 216.
57. See Armstrong, *In Search of Spiritual Power*, 82.
58. Arnott, *The Father's Blessing*, 43.
59. Arnott, *The Father's Blessing*, 20.
60. Arnott, *The Father's Blessing*, 20.

When Hysteria Becomes the Criteria

do you mean" intoned the pastor? The response from God actually "floored me," said the pastor. "Is it all right with you if I just love on my church for a while?" The Lord apparently responded.[61] The paradox is that, according to this kind of reasoning, it is better to have 80 percent of the church on the floor rolling around, and laughing while 99 percent of the world remains lost, and outside the church. Indeed, this is strange reasoning for a pastor. As evident earlier, it appears that many in the Vineyard movement agreed, severing ties with the church.

So, do most third-wave churches focus primarily on ecstatic phenomena at the cost of a sound gospel message? One author, Dager, seems to think so. He explained, referring to occurrences such as the Toronto Blessing that this so-called revival:

> has not come through the preaching of the gospel, but through allegedly uncontrollable laughter. Strange that Scripture doesn't record any such event. The apostles did perform signs and wonders, but the gospel was always clearly delineated, and repentance was called for. Seldom, if ever, is this the case with holy laughter.[62]

Another example of the displacing of the gospel is an anecdote told by Erwin Lutzer, a previous pastor of the Moody Church in Chicago. He wrote about three authors who knew the charismatic movement "inside out," and were mostly sympathetic to charismatic-type phenomena. However, they spoke of their "grave misgivings" about the occurrences during the Toronto Blessing in 1994. One of these pastors, Peter Fenwick, explained that his greatest fear is that the Bible no longer has the place it once did among evangelical Christians. Indeed, the whole controversy surrounding the Toronto Blessing is what he termed a "major battle for the Bible."[63]

---

61. Arnott, *The Father's Blessing*, 20.
62. Dager, *Holy Laughter*, 2.
63. Fenwick, *Prophecy Today*, lines 18–34.

The Pentecostal Paradox

Much of this, continued Fenwick, has "either no biblical foundation or only very dubious" ones.[64] Sadly, these types of practices now form a normal part of much of the charismatic teaching today. It seems, from the above observations, that such practices occur because of a lack of a biblical foundation within the churches involved in such phenomena. Accordingly, Synan, a well-known Pentecostal historian, agreed when commenting on similar occurrences (to be discussed later) during church meetings held in Lakeland, Florida, in 2008. In his own words, he sensed that there was "little scriptural foundation" present during the meetings he had witnessed.[65]

GOING FOR GOLD

It is indeed puzzling why the third-wave phenomenon continues to gain such unquestionable and uncritical acceptance among charismatic communities. Ostensibly, it seems that the esoteric experiences offered by these types of movements remain relatively popular. Is this, in part, because of the Third Wave movement's ability to recreate itself? Indeed, their leaders seem adept at adding new and exciting phases to the dying embers of the movement. This is especially so when the miracles begin to fade and, to keep their members from losing interest, a variety of new and seemingly miraculous things purportedly occur. A good example of this appeared toward the end of the 1990s. At this time, many believed that God was doing something new. Only this time, wonders such as gold fillings miraculously appeared in people's teeth. In fact, one Pentecostal leader, speaking to *Christianity Today*, affirmed that God was "up to something new," after reports surfaced from the TAV that gold fillings miraculously appeared in the teeth of some church members. The magazine asked whether God really did miraculously transform "dental amalgam fillings into gold?"[66]

---

64. Fenwick, *Prophecy Today*, lines 18–34.
65. Synan, *An Eyewitness Remembers*, 169.
66. Beverley, "Dental Miracle Reports," lines 1–16.

Unsurprisingly, reports of such phenomena drew significant criticism, with some viewing these occurrences as unbiblical, while others regarded such events simply as a "trivial pursuit" after the flames of the Toronto Blessing had died down. In the end, however, as expected, most of these claims remained unverified or were eventually debunked.[67] Later, the Toronto-based church admitted that it is yet to document any cases of such phenomena. Further, the leader of the church, where the supposed transforming of dental amalgam into gold occurred, explained, "we don't need to prove them, but I don't want to be a false witness to God."[68] On a lighter note, the pastor remarked, "this new thing is a miracle you don't have to be sick to get."[69]

In a sense, Armstrong was right when he asked, "where are the classes that Jesus' followers took in order to learn the skills necessary to fill teeth, lengthen legs, to smell God?" Indeed, continued Armstrong, "advanced courses in healing are offered, as though it were training in the magical arts."[70] As bizarre as these claims sound, as will become clear later, this type of reasoning forms a major plank in third-wave teaching. However, as Jurgensmeier insightfully explained, it is not "charismatic miracles," that God wants to achieve in people's lives today, but rather "character miracles."[71] Referring to such unusual phenomena, especially during the Toronto Blessing, a Regent College professor, in *Christianity Today*, claimed the church had "reached a new low allowing such anti-intellectualism and sectarianism that has plagued the Pentecostal and charismatic movements from their beginnings."[72]

---

67. Melton, Dentistry Paranormal. 88.
68. Beverley, "Dental Miracle Reports," lines 1–16.
69. Beverley, "Dental Miracle Reports," lines 1–16.
70. See Armstrong, *In Search of Spiritual Power*, 76.
71. Jurgensmeier, *Book 5 Apologetics*, 185.
72. Beverley, "Dental Miracle Reports," lines 21–24.

BLUNTING THE BLESSING OF THE BIBLE

Given the varying levels of hysteria occurring mostly within the Third Wave movement, a question worth pondering at this stage is whether this quest for more power is the best method of presenting the gospel. Or as mentioned before, does it distract from or even displace the main message of the gospel? Such an approach was evident in the 1980s book *Power Evangelism*, authored by the late John Wimber. This work aimed to emphasize signs of the miraculous as a way of declaring the gospel. As such, the preferred method of presenting a Bible-based message, according to this type of logic, is when people fall over (i.e., are slain in the Spirit—a phenomenon that will feature shortly) and teeth are filled with nothing less—of course than pure gold.[73] These rather bizarre forms of gospel presentation have unfortunately become a major plank among contemporary proponents of the Third Wave movement. However, as will become clear, this form of so-called "Power Evangelism, which they tout is hardly evangelism at all. Third Wave methodology," explained MacArthur, "seriously blunts the force of the gospel."[74] Part of the reason third-wave methodology blunts or dulls the force of the gospel is because of a continual quest for more power. Poloma stated, "the story of the revival and its attendant strange manifestations at TACF begins with its pastor, [and his wife] . . . and their quest for more of the power of the Holy Spirit."[75]

SLAIN IN THE SPIRIT

One sign many acknowledge as a token of God's favor (outside of the salvation of souls, of course), is being supposedly slain in the Spirit. This phenomenon occurs when the recipient enters another sort of consciousness (although not unconscious) and then

---

73. Lutzer, *Who You to Judge*, 118.
74. Macarthur, *Charismatic Chaos*, 164.
75. Poloma, *Main Street Mystics*, 60.

collapses "through a mere gesture or suggestion" explained Cottrell.[76] This and other types of phenomena, especially within third-wave circles, represent a "paradigm shift of major proportions" being promoted by some of the most prominent names within the Christian church, who "are endorsing this paradigm shift," noted Hanegraaff, "with little or no reservation."[77]

This is particularly relevant today, as Christianity is undergoing a shift from "faith to feelings, from fact to fantasy, and from reason to esoteric revelation."[78] Often, as is the case with such purported miracles, the non-Christian is healed and slain in the Spirit and saved all this, however, with just a token knowledge of the gospel.[79]

A good example of this is acknowledged by Torrey (see chapter 8), who noted the lack of decorum in some of the early Pentecostal meetings at the Azusa Street Mission in 1906. Apparently, "both men and women [were] lying on the floor in some sort of hypnotic state for hours on end."[80] Likewise, Larkin observed that the "conduct of those thus possessed, in which they fall to the ground and writhe in contortions . . . is more characteristic of 'demon possession' than a work of the Holy Spirit."[81] Another early Pentecostal leader, Parham, who originated the tongues phenomenon, commented on those among the early Pentecostals, whom he noted would sometimes fall under the power of God. In response to this phenomenon, Parham clearly stated:

> I know that people sometimes fall under the power of God, and there are times that God thus deals with his creatures that resist him; but these cases are exceptional, and not general. The falling under the power at

---

76. Cottrell, *The Holy Spirit*, 112.
77. Hanegraaff, *Counterfeit Revival*, 9.
78. Hanegraaff, *Counterfeit Revival*, 9.
79. See Armstrong, *In Search of Spiritual Power*, 82.
80. Torrey, "The Kings Business," 362.
81. Larkin, *Dispensational Truth*, 102–103.

Los Angeles [Azusa Street], has, to a large degree, been produced through a hypnotic, mesmeric, magnetic current.[82]

Despite some obvious differences between Parham and his protégé Seymour, these statements should give pause for thought given that these words came not from an outsider, but the purported founder of Pentecostalism. Significantly, Parham suggested that "those who resist" are the ones who ultimately "fall under the power."[83]

This current practice, in some areas of the church—falling under the power or becoming slain in the Spirit—is at times referred to in Pentecostal circles as "carpet time." As will become clear later, this type of phenomenon is more common in today's church than ever before, especially among third-wave Pentecostals. Therefore, an interesting question to ponder at this point may be, is there any biblical/historical warrant for being slain in the Spirit?

In trying to prove the emphasis of these claims, a book was published at the height of the Toronto Blessing in the 1990s, titled *Catch the Fire*. This work asserted, among other things, a claim that those who fall over during meetings can apparently find justification for this experience in Psalm 23. The author stated that those who have "done 'carpet time' at the Airport [Church] have a frame of reference for much of what is declared in the Psalm, not the least being the dynamic of verse 2: he makes me lie down. . .!"[84] Much of this Psalm is, of course, intended as a source of comfort and strength for the reader. However, Bible verses can easily be twisted to fit and/or justify a phenomenon that appears to have little or no precedent in the Bible. Another example of using Scripture to justify strange phenomena occurred when (as mentioned earlier) there were claims made of gold fillings miraculously appearing in people's teeth. All this was happening just as the Toronto Blessing began to wind down. Apparently, those within the church leadership team could find a verse in the Bible to fit the phenomenon.

82. Parham, *The Life of Charles Parham*, 169.
83. Parham, *The Life of Charles Parham*, 169.
84. Chevreau, *Catch the Fire*, 51.

The verse used? Well, they believed that God, when performing these types of miracles, was keeping the promise of Psalm 81:10, in which it says, "open your mouth wide, and I will fill it."[85]

In reality, encounters such as falling over or being "Slain in the Spirit" occurred in biblical times. However, this phenomenon only usually took place in personal encounters with God. The only difference is that on these occasions, the recipients did not have someone praying for them who, in turn, generally fell over (with a catcher surreptitiously standing behind them ready to lower them to the floor). Again, nowhere in the Bible is this modern interpretation of being slain in the Spirit mentioned. Accordingly, MacArthur stated that this phenomenon was "a modern charismatic invention. This practice is mentioned nowhere in the Bible; it is completely without scriptural warrant."[86] Indeed, continued MacArthur:

> the modern phenomenon has become such a common and popular spectacle that the average charismatic today takes it for granted, assuming it must have some kind of clear biblical or historical pedigree. But not only is the phenomenon completely absent from the biblical record of the early church; it has nothing whatsoever to do with the Holy Spirit.[87]

There is no record, states Pullum, in the entire text of the Bible that anyone ever "shook, laughed or cried uncontrollably, trembled, collapsed on the floor, or fell backward to the ground" as if being slain in the Spirit, as some in today's contemporary church would have us believe.[88] As such, the contemporary phenomenon of being, "slain in the spirit," mused Lutzer, "is not only absent in Scripture, it is contrary to the kinds of ministries done by Christ and the Apostles."[89]

---

85. Beverley, "Dental Miracle Reports," lines 1–16.
86. MacArthur, *Strange Fire*, 199.
87. MacArthur, *Strange Fire*, 199.
88. Pullum, *Faith Healers and the Bible*, 131.
89. Lutzer, *Who Are You to Judge*, 101.

SHAKTIPAT HIT THE MAT

Much of the Pentecostal practice of falling over (yes, to an extent, tongues, healing, etc.), similarly occurs in pagan cultures and pseudo-religions. Let me explain what I mean. In Hinduism, a term often used is "Shaktipat." The root of the suffix "Pata" means to fall. In this pseudo-religious practice, a so-called "guru" would place their hands on a follower. They usually perform this practice through physical touch. Then, grace is supposedly imparted, which in Hinduism apparently triggers the gradual awakening of the Kundalini, producing various physical and emotional phenomena. Some of these manifestations included, among other things, "uncontrollable laughing, roaring, barking, hissing, crying, and shaking."[90] It is clear that the source and formula of the Hindu origin of this phenomenon are on a completely different level to the current Pentecostal/charismatic-type aspects. Further, it does not follow that Pentecostalism patterns itself along the same lines. However, given the lack of biblical and historical support for this activity, it certainly should raise a red flag about whether such events are an authentic practice. Or indeed, whether such manifestations, even belong in the Christian church at all. Although parallels between various religious phenomena do not always share the same source, it is important to note that partaking of experience does not necessarily confirm the practice. There were, indeed, descriptions of manifestations of various kinds occurring in church history and the biblical text. However, we must keep in mind that those who fell over in biblical times did so only under deep conviction of sin. It may be also worth noting that practices such as being slain in the Spirit were discouraged given that they often detracted from the message of the gospel. Finally, these types of phenomena did not occur because some evangelist jolted them with spiritual power. However, most importantly, such occurrences were never publicly shown, encouraging others to share the same experience.[91]

---

90. Smith, "Holy Laughter or Strong Delusion?" lines 1–6.
91. Smith, "Holy Laughter or Strong Delusion?" lines 1–6.

In sharp contrast to the above, one of the largest Pentecostal groups today, the AG, interestingly enough holds an official position on this phenomenon. In trying to prove what they describe as "extra-biblical manifestations," they have outlined specific guidelines. The following terms used by the organization are, unusual to say the least, and include such phenomena as being, "slain in the Spirit," "falling under the power," or "resting in the Spirit." At the same time, while freely using these phrases, the organization admits that these terms do not actually appear in the Bible. Such terms are used; however, the organization affirmed, "to describe the experience of falling to the floor under the power of the Holy Spirit."[92] Despite the lack of biblical support for the practice, the AG still recognizes such phenomena. On a more positive note, the organization rightly states, "overwhelming experiences, such as falling to the floor, are, therefore, in themselves not to be encouraged as a pattern."[93] However, ironically, they further state that a "courtesy fall is never the work of the Spirit, nor is a quick rise so others may have the experience."[94] Again, there is no reference made to any Bible verse for such phenomena, simply because Scripture does not condone these types of practices. One would need to delve deep into church history to even find a hint of such things occurring.

IS GOD DOING SOMETHING NEW?

As this chapter has reflected on the various phenomena purportedly occurring within the Third Wave movement, the question to ponder is whether God is doing something new within this group, and if so, what is that "something new?" Well, this is a highly debatable subject and often in the case with purported phenomena,

---

92. Assemblies of God, "Manifestations of the Spirit," lines 5–10.
93. Assemblies of God, "Manifestations of the Spirit," lines 5–10.
94. Assemblies of God, "Manifestations of the Spirit," lines 5–10.

as Lutzer rightly stated, "sound biblical interpretation is thrown aside in favor of the 'new thing' God is doing."[95]

What is true, however, is the fact that these so-called supernatural experiences are, in reality, nothing new. Indeed, the time-tested Bible truths, which affirm, "there is no new thing under the sun" (Ecclesiastes 1:9) still hold true today.[96] Therefore, ecstatic experiences are nothing new, explained Johns, "in spite of the constant reminders that God is doing a new thing in our time . . . it is not an original script."[97] As we will see later, this aspect of sensationalism and emotive behavior, broadly speaking, is not something new within the Third Wave movement. In fact, among this group, "bizarre doctrines and behavior have become so commonplace," explained MacArthur, "that they hardly make headlines anymore."[98] Throughout history, many have taught various things resembling this aspect of ecstatic phenomena. For example, a group called the Montanists, a radical, fly-by-night mystical group, originated in AD 156. The sect, according to Bruner, was "the fountainhead of all the enthusiastic or pneumatic [spiritual] movements in Christian history." Interestingly, Bruner noted the "striking similarities, in almost every point," between this group and modern-day Pentecostalism.[99] The reasons for the similarities, according to Bruner, are the following. First, they assumed that the last period of revelation had (then) started; second, and more notably, they held a distinctive emphasis on the Holy Spirit; and the third main aspect is either ecstasy or excitement, which often forms a significant part of the Pentecostal experience.[100] So, is Montanism a model to follow? Undoubtedly not. The leader of this group, Montanus, according to Eusebius, "became beside himself

---

95. Lutzer, *Who Are You to Judge*, 101.
96. NKJV.
97. Johns, *The Pentecostal Paradigm*, 24.
98. MacArthur, *Strange Fire*, 6.
99. Bruner, *A Theology of the Holy Spirit*, 36.
100. Bruner, *A Theology of the Holy Spirit*, 36.

WHEN HYSTERIA BECOMES THE CRITERIA

and being suddenly in a sort of frenzy and ecstasy, he raved and began to babble and utter strange things."[101]

Further, this type of teaching of ecstatic phenomena is nothing new within the history of the church. In fact, "in the early years of the church" wrote Johns, "this type of teaching was dominant among Corinthian believers."[102] Of course, the Corinthian Church is the only example we have, outside the book of Acts of speaking in tongues. So, are they a good model for the church to follow also?

SEIZED WITH A SPOOK

As sad as it is, these "exotic practices" are not only confined to the Third Wave movement, the reality is; however, these types of phenomena go all the way back to the Azusa Street Mission in 1906. An example of this is detailed in a sad tale told by Charles Parham (arguably the progenitor of Pentecostalism). He draws a vivid description of such strange phenomena occurring in early Pentecostal meetings in a book titled *The Life of Charles Parham*. It tells of a Methodist Minister whom Parham described in his own words as being, "seized with a spook" after attending one of the Azusa Street meetings. Upon returning home, he had a hollow stare in his eyes. Standing at the window, he would bark like a dog. Parham related that he would go into the mountains hoping to get relief through prayer. Instead, he would suddenly begin to "bray like a donkey or crow like a rooster." At last, his mother-in-law, upon her deathbed uttered her last prayer on this earth, which was for his freedom. Parham then states that after getting relief the man "went on after that to live a normal life."[103]

What then were some of these early Pentecostal meetings like? Pentecostal author Robeck describes the events at the Azusa Street meetings stating they not only "spoke in tongues, prophesied, preached divine healing, but they went into trances, saw

---

101. Pamphilus, *The Sacred Writings of Eusebius*, 164.
102. Johns, *The Pentecostal Paradigm*, 24.
103. Parham, *The Everlasting Gospel*, 86.

visions, and engaged in other phenomena such as jumping, rolling, laughing, shouting, barking, and falling under the power of the Holy Spirit."[104]

Having looked at various phenomena associated primarily within the Third Wave movement; the next section will visit two other scenes that displayed aspects similar to the 1994 Toronto Blessing. These events were at both the Brownsville AG in Pensacola, in 1998, and later in Lakeland, Florida, in 2008.

THE NEXT WAVE TO LAP THE PENTECOSTAL SHORES

The next waves to appear after the Toronto Blessing were not long in coming. Hard on the heels of the Toronto events, a similar phenomenon arrived on the scene. Only this time, it appeared in the Brownsville AG Church in Pensacola, Florida, on Father's Day, June 18, 1995. Similar occurrences to those of the earlier Toronto episode were on display, with the usual shaking, laughing, and rolling on the floor. Again, another similar event took place in the AG Church, Lakeland, Florida, in 2008. One point to remember is that the AG was favorable toward some of these more esoteric forms of Christianity. Writing in *Christianity Today* in 1998, General Superintendent of the AG Thomas Trask, in an article titled The Brownsville Revival Rolls Onward, made some startling comments. Trask inferred that the impact of the Brownsville AG Church events had "been powerful." Indeed, Trask continued, "many, many of our pastors, have gone [to Brownsville] searching, looking, and believing, and they have witnessed the power of God. It has done something for their own hearts and lives."[105] What it had done in the hearts and lives of others remains open to debate, leaving many unanswered questions. In fact, it is on record that some 122,000 decision cards came to officials at the Brownsville, Pensacola Church, indicating either conversion or re-dedication.

---

104. Robeck, *The Azusa Street* Mission, 12.
105. Rabey, "Brownsville Revival," lines 22–30.

Further, over two million visitors attended the meetings during the late 1990s.[106] So, what happened to the 122,000 new inquirers? Most of these "people have been leaving for three or four years," the pastor told me [editor Lee Grady]. "Some are not in church at all, including some who were on staff. I don't know anyone who has not been hurt."[107]

Where, however, is that same Pensacola Church today? An article written one-decade post-Pensacola in *Charisma* magazine told the sad tale of the state of this church. The report asked some searching questions, such as why "the church that hosted hundreds of thousands of visitors has shrunk to a few hundred members, and now owes millions of dollars for a building they can't fill." Further, the author struggles "to understand why so many people who once were part of the Brownsville Church now feel hurt and betrayed?"[108]

To make matters worse, the leader of the church resigned in 2003, starting a new church just 50 miles away from the Pensacola Church. Soon, the latest pastor resigned as the church "dipped below 400" members, with a large portion of the members of the Brownsville church attending a local Southern Baptist church, while "many others don't go anywhere." [109]

LAUGHING IN LAKELAND

After this episode, a similar situation exploded onto the scene, only this time it occurred at Ignited Church, Lakeland, Florida on April 2, 2008. Once again, the events occurred at AG-hosted meetings. At that time, various articles appeared during its short tenure. Few actually extolled its virtues. However, one review in particular—written by a well-known charismatic magazine—is worth examining in some detail. From this article, it seems safe to assume that

---

106. Rabey, "Brownsville Revival," lines 22–30.
107. Grady, "What Happened to Brownsville's Fire?" lines 60–65.
108. Grady, "What Happened to Brownsville's Fire?" lines 30–35.
109. Grady, "What Happened to Brownsville's Fire?" lines 55–62.

some interesting questions remain unanswered. In addition, some questions posed by the magazine are perplexing, to say the least. After experiencing the events at this Lakeland church, the author felt the entire audience should have run for the exits, after witnessing the strange goings-on. The editor further mused:

> why didn't anyone correct the error from the pulpit? After all, godly leaders are supposed to protect the sheep from heresy, not spoon feed deception to them. Only God knows how far this poison traveled from Lakeland to take root elsewhere. May God forgive us for allowing his word to be so flippantly contaminated.[110]

This article, although now unavailable online through *Charisma* magazine (despite the author's attempts) raises some serious questions not addressed by the Pentecostal movement. One of these questions, for instance, relates to who ensures that such activities do not occur again. Additionally, and more importantly, what safeguards are in place to ensure those in authority continue to, as the previous article put it, "protect the sheep from heresy, not spoon feed deception to them."[111]

RUN FOR THE EXITS

Similarly, Pentecostal historian Vinson Synan sensed that "something didn't ring true" about what occurred at the Lakeland AG Church.[112] Although the author did not attend these meetings and experience the events firsthand, interestingly, he claims to have viewed it all from the vantage point of television. Nevertheless, there was a sense, even viewing the occurrences from this perspective, of the dire lack of a Bible-based foundation in the meetings. Due to the perceived lack of substance on display at the Lakeland meetings, the author reluctantly admitted that, in the end, it seemed to "cast a pall over similar revivals" that might in the future

---

110. Grady, "Life after Lakeland," lines 1–20.
111. Grady, "Life after Lakeland," lines 1–20.
112. Synan, *An Eyewitness Remembers*, 169.

grace the Pentecostal Shores.[113] Ironically, the same author seemed to suggest that these events might even become a footnote to the first two revivals, which occurred almost simultaneously (i.e., Brownsville and Toronto). However, it would seem the footnote should actually read, "run for the exits," if we are to take notice of the *Charisma* article covering the Lakeland events.

Ironically, in terms of the Lakeland events, one Pentecostal historian wrote, "in the end; my sense is that the Toronto and Brownsville revivals, which were practically simultaneous in time, could well go down in history as parts of another great awakening in the style of the Cane Ridge and Azusa Street revivals."[114] In all, the occurrences at the Lakeland Church lasted only a few months, from April to October 2008. Thankfully, since 2008, this type of Pentecostal phenomena seems not to have taken root elsewhere.

Sadly, there has been a multitude of advocates claiming that these types of Pentecostal phenomena resemble true revival. Although with the advantage of hindsight, it is evident that while many seem to testify to the effectiveness of these so-called "revivals," the outcome leaves much to be desired. After all, given that laughter and not deep repentance, appears to be the main characteristic of these manifestations, perhaps it is safe to assume that rather than being a launching point for revival, these types of phenomena have instead become a laughing point in the eyes of a watching world. Take the so-called Toronto Blessing for example; what has it left in its wake? The events in Toronto, Brownsville and later at Lakeland seem to suggest that many Pentecostals are comfortable with the status quo of the movement today. The prevailing attitude, at least on the surface, is oh well; Christ may be coming soon, but maybe not. Therefore, wrote Cox, "nothing will interrupt their pursuit of success and self-indulgence. The Kingdom Now movement and the name-it-and-claim-it preachers have elevated this complacency into a theology."[115]

---

113. Synan, *An Eyewitness Remembers*, 169.
114. Synan, *An Eyewitness Remembers*,169.
115. Cox, *Fire from Heaven*, 317–18.

THE PROSPERITY PHENOMENON

There has been a plethora of commentary presented in the news media and elsewhere about a new wave surging through the church. Often, however, this type of Christianity is branded the "prosperity gospel." Most of these reports, while sometimes focusing on the more controversial aspects of the new "faith movement," undoubtedly seem to pay attention to some of the most unacceptable tendencies creeping into this movement. Sadly, media reports seem to focus primarily on a minority group within Pentecostalism, "whose most visible leaders—televangelists, faith healers, self-proclaimed prophets, and prosperity preachers boldly claim his name while," as MacArthur lamented, "simultaneously dragging it through the mud."[116] A good example of this is a comment picked up by the *New York Times* that highlights one of these prosperity preachers. The picture painted is of an appeal given to the faithful while standing on a platform "before thousands of believers weighed down by debt and economic insecurity."[117] The event occurred just after what is commonly known as the Global Financial Crisis or GFC. Amid this economic downturn, the prosperity preacher assured the faithful in the audience that, "God knows where the money is, and he knows how to get the money to you."[118] Now, I am sure that God knows where the money is. However, according to the above statement, it seems that the prosperity message is aimed primarily at those who prefer their wallets to bulge and not their souls to prosper. Therefore, a pertinent question at this point is this; does the prosperity message resonate with the average Christian? Indeed, this question remains open to debate given the stark reality that, according to statisticians (the late) David Barrett and Todd Johnson, at least 87 percent of all Christians live below the poverty line. These figures, although taken in 2001, show that a sizeable part of Pentecostalism is within the developing world. For example, some 29 percent of Pentecostals are white, while 71

---

116. MacArthur, *Strange Fire*, 5.
117. Goodstein, "Believers Invest," lines 1–22.
118. Goodstein, "Believers Invest," lines 1–22.

percent are of different ethnicity, making up the global picture of the worldwide story of Pentecostalism.[119]

Given the above statistics, much of the prosperity movement's formula may well not be as effective in the life of the average Christian as some seem to suggest. From a demographical point of view, in North America at least, most Christians live in the least wealthy states. There is, of course, no way of determining how many Christians actually hold to prosperity-type teaching. However, as a way of testing the so-called prosperity gospel hypotheses, Barbare, in his book *The 80% Solution,* described a survey aimed at grasping how widespread this type of teaching is in the US. The study, conducted by Fitzpatrick compared two specific measures. First, the *American Religious Identification Survey* (ARIS) 2008 was consulted. This was a good barometer of the number of how many Christians lived within the forty-eight states surveyed. Next, this information was compared to the average median income test measured by government sources from 2005 onward. Predictably, the results revealed that states with the highest proportion of Christians had the lowest median income. While the research "leaves plenty of room for speculation," explained Barbare, "and does not isolate Prosperity Christians, it is a starting point."[120]

Given that the prosperity message appears not to have resonated with the average Christian, it does seem to have transferred success to those who proclaim the prosperity message. As a case in point, in November 2007, a US Senate finance committee established an inquiry. The purpose was to gauge just how wealthy some prominent Pentecostal personalities were. The probe sought to delve into the finances of six of the best-known names in televangelism to decide whether there was any financial impropriety or violation of their tax-exempt status. In most instances, they seem to have escaped any penalty in the inquiry; however, a cloud still hangs over this type of message, especially with the publicity generated by such an investigation. As a result, according to an *NBC* report, some questions may never be answered, including

---

119. Barrett, *World Christian Trends,* 284.
120. Barbare, *The 80% Solution,* 287.

The Pentecostal Paradox

queries about the "personal use of church-owned airplanes, luxury homes and credit cards by pastors and their families." Another key concern regarded the "lack of oversight of finances by boards often packed with the televangelists' relatives and friends."[121]

Having explored the general appeal or lack thereof, of the prosperity gospel formula, an appropriate question at this point may be how many Christians actually follow this formula as a part of their faith and practice? It seems, on the surface at least, that this teaching is still very prevalent throughout the Pentecostal movement. For example, around 90 percent of Christians polled in a Pew Forum survey (out of ten countries), claimed to believe God would grant material prosperity to all believers if they only had enough faith.[122] In stark contrast to this, a more evangelical group of delegates to a Lausanne Congress of World Evangelism, convened in Cape Town in 2010, found that only 7 percent of respondents surveyed believed that God grants wealth and good health to those with enough faith.[123] Although these types of figures seem to bear out, the reality is that the so-called prosperity gospel is making inroads into certain sectors of Pentecostalism. However, it certainly by no means clearly defined as to how many adhere to this type of message. An approximate indication of the prevalence of this teaching, though, can be gained from a 2006 *Time* magazine article, suggestively titled, "Does God Want you to be Rich?" According to this report, around 17 percent of respondents stated they adhered to the prosperity-type of belief.

Further, about two-thirds—or at least 61 percent—believed that God wanted Christians to become prosperous. Additionally, a further 31 percent agreed that if you give, you will get more.[124] According to such statistics, the operative word, it would seem is "more."

---

121. Zoll, "Televangelists Escape Penalty," lines 5–11.
122. PEW Research Center, "Spirit and Power," 9.
123. Offutt, *New Centers of Global Evangelicalism*, 149.
124. Van Biema et al., "Does God Want You to Be Rich?" 50.

THE POPULARITY OF PROSPERITY PREACHING

Part of the broad appeal of the prosperity gospel lies in the brands it boasts. For example, one thinks of such formulas as Name it and Claim it, the Word of Faith Movement, and so on. This becomes only too evident when surveying the titles of many popular books that line Christian bookstore shelves. Consider, for example, some book titles from the Word of Faith Movement, which tends to suggest a health and wealth type of gospel: *How to Write Your Own Ticket with God*,[125] *The Force of Faith*,[126] and so on. This kind of thinking seems to promote the view that prosperity is within the grasp of anybody with enough faith.

Now that we have seen the prosperity message's popularity among Christians; next, it might be useful to look at a few terms that are used by the Christian community and the broader world as well. Surprisingly, although the prosperity message remains relatively popular among certain segments of Christianity, its broad appeal, or the lack thereof, does not seem to extend to the media. For example, *Christianity Today* termed prosperity preaching an "aberrant theology that teaches God rewards faith."[127] *The Washington Post* deemed the prosperity message as little more than a "vapid bless-me club," and an "insipid heresy." the article went even further even describing prosperity teaching as one of the "worst ideas of the decade" leading up to the end of the twentieth century. This message, the Post maintained amounts to "little more than spiritual, magical thinking: If you pray the right way, God will make you rich."[128]

The Billy Graham-affiliated Lausanne conference, speaking of the prosperity gospel issued an apt description of prosperity teaching as being a "false and grave distortion of the Bible."[129] Further, the statement affirmed that this kind of practice was not

---

125. Hagin, *How to Write Your Own Ticket*.
126. Copeland, *The Force of Faith*.
127. *Christianity Today*, "Prosperity Gospel," line 1.
128. Falsani,"The Worst Ideas of the Decade," lines 7–30.
129. Lausanne,"Prosperity Gospel," line 20.

only unethical but more significantly, offers no lasting hope. More worryingly, it could; the report continued, "deflect people from the main message, the only means of eternal salvation." In such terms, the Lausanne movement further stated that the prosperity gospel "can be soberly described as a false gospel."[130]

Mohler believes that the prosperity-type teaching where many seem to think that God grants, financial favors to his people along with bodily health is a "false Gospel that turns the Gospel of Christ upside-down."[131] Smith further asserted that the "what-you-say is-what-you-get teaching, otherwise known as the Prosperity Gospel . . . sound (s) more like Mary Baker Eddie [the progenitor of the Scientist, Church of Christ] than the Apostle Paul."[132]

---

130. Lausanne, "Prosperity Gospel," line 20.
131 Mohler, "News Note," lines 60–65.
132. Smith, *Charisma vs. Charismania*, 135.

5

Toggling Tongues

A "WEIRD BABEL OF Tongues," read the blazing headlines of the *Los Angeles Daily Times*, April 18, 1906.[1] The article described a new fledgling religious movement appearing on the scene with words like "a new sect of fanatics breaking loose," and, "wild scene last night on Azusa Street." It described the phenomenon of speaking in tongues, which was apparent at the meetings, as a "gurgle of wordless talks" and, "mouthing a creed which it would seem no sane mortal could understand."[2] The notoriety of this type of publicity only fanned the flame, and soon news of a new Pentecostal movement breaking out at the Azusa Street Mission spread everywhere. The result was that people from across the US—and even the world—headed to Azusa Street trying to "catch the fire."[3] Such were the beginnings of the Pentecostal movement that the *Los Angeles Daily Times* described as, "the newest religious sect that began in Los Angeles."[4]

---

1. *Los Angeles Times*, "Weird Babel of Tongues," 1.
2. *Los Angeles Times*, "Weird Babel of Tongues," 1.
3. Hanegraaff, *Counterfeit Revival*, 127.
4. *Los Angeles Times*, "Weird Babel of Tongues," 1.

PARHAM'S VIEW ON THE TONGUES PHENOMENON

Ecstatic speech or the tongues phenomenon often characterizes the Pentecostal movement; given this, you would expect this aspect to become a uniting factor of the movement. However, as you read on, it will become increasingly clear that divisions brewed over the issue of speaking in tongues from some within the burgeoning Pentecostal movement even in its earliest stages. Adding fuel to an already smoldering fire, the originator of the movement, Parham, painted a stark picture of the tongues phenomenon that he had helped to originate. In fact, Parham, who had his own inimitable way of phrasing things, recorded his thoughts on the Pentecostal movement in a book titled *The Everlasting Gospel*.[5] Although he wrote this book in 1911, the publication was delayed until at least the 1920s.[6] The following excerpts from this book may seem a little caustic to the average reader. However, as this chapter will later show, Parham's views on the tongues phenomenon differed vastly from the opinions of most of his fellow Pentecostals. For example, in the above book, Parham estimated that at "least two-thirds of this tongue stuff over the country is not Pentecost."[7] In his mind, at least, the Pentecostals had not produced the goods, and accordingly, he claimed that most, "religious leaders and teachers condemn the work wholesale."[8] Compounding the issue further, he later became even more adamant, when reiterating his earlier claim. This time, however, he has increased his estimate. Parham stated that in his opinion, at least "three-fourths" of those within the Pentecostal movement as he phrased it were, "counterfeits."[9] If this were not enough, on the practice of speaking in tongues, he wrote:

---

5. Parham, *The Everlasting Gospel*.
6. Oliverio, *Theological Hermeneutics*, 52.
7. Parham, *The Everlasting Gospel*, 48.
8. Parham, *The Everlasting Gospel*, 86.
9. Parham, *The Everlasting Gospel*, 71.

> By the Baptism with the Holy Spirit, I do not mean all the chattering and jabbering, wind-sucking, holy-dancing-rollerism, going on all over the country, which is the result of hypnotic spiritualistic and fleshly controls . . . a real sane reception of the Holy Spirit in baptismal power, filling you with glory unspeakable and causing you, without any effort, to speak freely in foreign languages this is called the sealing.[10]

Part of the reason he gave for his criticisms of the movement was that, in his estimation, followers had become deluded because of an "unteachable spirit and their fanatical zeal," in what he called the "propagation of falsities." Further, he contemptuously added, "God pity them!"[11]

From the above statements, it seems that the originator of Pentecostalism, Parham, came to reject outright what most Pentecostals eventually accepted—that those speaking in tongues were using heavenly—albeit unintelligible prayer languages.[12] Conversely, however, Parham also believed the Pentecostal practice of speaking in tongues should instead be a useful tool that people received for evangelism. In essence, the point Parham was trying to make was that the true meaning of speaking in tongues was a literal dialect spoken, "fluently and smoothly proven by some disinterested foreigner witnessing to the fact that they really used a language."[13] Increasingly, it seems that Parham viewed the new Pentecostal movement as being out-of-step with his teaching; however, the main concern was the definition and practice of speaking in tongues. Accordingly, the original meaning and purpose of speaking in tongues ought to be in the context of foreign missionary work. In this way, the recipients of this phenomenon would then play a useful role in ushering in an end-time revival. Initially, many Pentecostal missionaries agreed with Parham's view that speaking in tongues was a literal, or at least a genuine

10. Parham, *The Everlasting Gospel*, 71.
11. Parham, *The Everlasting Gospel*, 71.
12. Walsh, *Pentecostals in America*, 86.
13. Parham, *The Everlasting Gospel*, 86.

foreign language. However, even this teaching proved unfounded, as various attempts by early Pentecostals to use what they believed to be divinely received native languages in the foreign missionary field, ultimately failed. It was not long before most, if not all, of the Pentecostals except Parham discovered that this was not the case after all. Soon, the realization dawned that the adherents had not received knowledge of any known foreign language. Instead, they were speaking indecipherable words. To complicate matters further, the confusion over speaking in tongues only increased with Parham rejecting the current Pentecostal view of the practice.

Furthermore, as will become clear later, the original idea of tongues being a foreign language fell thoroughly into disrepute as the two leaders, Parham and Seymour, eventually clashed over the issue. Therefore, it was not long after the launch of the new Pentecostal movement before cracks appeared in the movement's structure. Before long, things became increasingly fraught and tense.

In a sense, the leader of the movement, Seymour would eventually adopt a different stance on the tongues issue than most Pentecostals would be comfortable with today. He believed that becoming preoccupied with any sign or gift was wrong, primarily when it concerned the so-called initial evidence of tongues so highly prized among Pentecostals, even to this day. Further, Seymour became convinced that if speaking in tongues was the only evidence of having received the Spirit baptism, this could ultimately open the door to deception (see chapter 8).[14] This warning is timely, given that within Pentecostal circles today, speaking in tongues alone is accepted as primary evidence of the baptism in the Holy Spirit. In the end, it seems Seymour grew increasingly impatient with dogmatic beliefs. Especially when it came to the insistence that speaking in tongues is the only real evidence of the baptism in the Holy Spirit. These factors prompted him to decide, for whatever reason, to reject Parham's original theory that speaking in tongues evidenced the Spirit baptism.[15]

---

14. See Robeck, "The Azusa Street Revival," 344–45.
15. See Espinosa, "Ordinary Prophet," 56.

SEYMOUR'S STANCE ON TONGUES CHANGES

Ironically, Seymour's stance on the meaning of speaking in tongues shifted dramatically at or around 1907.[16] This change meant that he no longer accepted the belief (still prevalent today in many Pentecostal circles) that tongues-speaking was biblical evidence of Spirit baptism. Ironically, it seems that Seymour's changed stance on this issue has not received broad recognition by most, if not all, Pentecostal leaders today. This is clear from a remark in a book titled *The Charismatic Century*. Oddly enough, in this work, Pentecostal authors Hayford and Moore concluded, "Seymour's moderated position on the evidential value of tongues wouldn't allow him to hold ministerial credentials in many Pentecostal denominations today."[17] Unsurprisingly, then, this view would place him at odds with many contemporary Pentecostal groups, most of whom still have as fundamental teaching that speaking in tongues is the real evidence of Spirit baptism. If the above statement were accurate, then they would exclude the movement's founder from becoming a minister in the organization he helped to establish! Ironically, even this belief is losing momentum today. As will become clear at the chapter's close, the phenomenon of speaking in tongues is rapidly decreasing in popularity among most Pentecostal groups worldwide.

TODAY'S VERSION OF TONGUES

As outlined in the earlier statements of the movement's founder Parham, it seems that today's version of tongues-speaking bears little or no resemblance to its original intention. This is especially pertinent given the status placed upon the practice in most Pentecostal churches. That is not to say, however, that the meaning of speaking in tongues is fully understood by those who take part in the Pentecostal movement today. In effect, few (if any) of those who practice this phenomenon would know of the significant shift

---

16. Synan and Fox, *William J. Seymour*, 311.
17. Hayford and Moore, *The Charismatic Century*, chapter 3.

it undertook during the movement's formative years, as the following story might relate.

In 1906, only months after the Azusa Street Mission's beginnings, a well-meaning couple A.G. Garr (1874–1944) and his wife Lillian embarked on the mission field. In fact, so convinced were they that their newly gained tongues experience was a literal foreign language, they set sail immediately for Calcutta, India. For the most part, they believed—just as many of the early Pentecostals had before them—that it was possible to bypass the arduous task of having to learn a foreign language. As a result of this seemingly over-optimistic view of the phenomenon, this young missionary couple presumptuously entered the mission field. Could it be, they thought this exciting new experience could speed up the missionary task? Later, upon arrival in India, they discovered that they had indeed been mistaken. In a sense, this experience is reminiscent of the well-known words of John Wesley: "I went to America to convert the Indians, but who will convert me?" Much to their chagrin, upon arrival in India, they discovered that they could not converse in the native language after all. Nevertheless, the most interesting part of the story has almost escaped our notice. Undeterred by their initial failure, the Garr's had a brilliant idea. Why not simply redefine the meaning of tongues?

TOGGLING TONGUES

From this moment, speaking in tongues within the Pentecostal movement would forever change. Now, the phenomenon seemed to take on an entirely new meaning, which in today's terms would amount to an unintelligible prayer language. The realization triggered this change in direction in that they could no longer continue with the phenomenon of speaking in tongues in its present state. As a result, they changed its meaning, so much so, MacArthur poignantly stated, "Charismatics and Pentecostals still cannot communicate with people from different language groups (or even with one another) unless they have learned whatever language they wish to use."[18] Now, instead of sticking with Parham's original theory, they conveniently "toggled" the meaning of speaking in tongues to suit their own purposes. As a result, the Garr's concluded that their newly found gift of speaking in tongues was not an earthly language after all. They now assumed it a heavenly or unique prayer language. Therefore, this ill-fated attempt at the missionary task led to entirely new teaching, which, on this scale, has been almost unknown in the church for the best part of 2,000 years.

In a sense, this redefinition of speaking in tongues satisfied an age-old quest—that is, the desire for physical proof of having received the Holy Spirit.[19] Simply put, early in their Calcutta experience, this aspiring missionary couple not only had to face the language gap, but they were also forced to re-examine and redefine the real meaning of speaking in tongues.[20] "Had Garr and the early Pentecostals not reformulated their experience of the Spirit," maintained Mittelstadt, "their interest in and employment of tongues would surely have declined."[21] As a result, if they had not reinvented the meaning of the tongues phenomenon, the Pentecostal movement may well not have eventuated at all, at least not in its present form.

Interestingly, however, as mentioned previously, Parham initially believed and taught that missionaries could go to the ends of the earth and miraculously speak fluently in unlearned human languages. It was not long, as Pentecostal historian Synan observed (in part, referring to the Garrs' unsuccessful attempt), before "all Pentecostals except Parham dropped this belief due to unsuccessful efforts at preaching in unknown tongues in India and other places."[22] Did all these failed attempts at missionary tongues distract Parham and the early Pentecostals from their purpose? Well, again, no. It is interesting, however, that even as late as 1919, over

18. MacArthur, "Tongue Tied," lines 10–12.
19. Kostlevy, *Holy Jumpers*, 132.
20. McGee, *The Calcutta Revival of 1907*, 125.
21. See Mittelstadt, *Reimaging Luke-Acts*, 28.
22. See Synan, *Parham, Charles Fox*, 753.

The Pentecostal Paradox

a decade after the aforementioned failed attempt at missionary work, Parham was still insistent that tongues were a foreign language. He claimed, "we have several missionaries in the field who have the gift of tongues, which not only speak the language and understand the natives but can use the language intelligently; it has become a gift to them."[23] How soon it became apparent to all that this view was incorrect. As a result, "by the beginning of the second generation," explained Pentecostal historian Wacker, "the concept of missionary tongues had receded into the hazy realm of Pentecostal mythology."[24] Yet, as noted in chapter 1, the folklore notion that first developed at the Azusa Street Mission in 1906 continues to self-perpetuate. Once more, a mythical understanding of the Bible leads to difficulties and disappointment. Indeed, even a casual glance at church history during the last century or so shows that this is a mistaken notion. Ultimately, the embarrassment over the foreign language debacle seemed to matter little to enthusiasts such as Garr, who ended up adopting a view that "would accommodate this frustrating realization."[25] Eventually, through force of circumstances—failure, or otherwise—they had to interpret the gift as speaking in unknown or unintelligible languages.[26] Accordingly, MacArthur perhaps summarized this situation best by stating that, "the movement Charles Parham helped start has grown to massive proportions today." Yet, in the light of such irrefutable evidence of the patent failure, not only of the so-called missionary tongues but also the controversies surrounding Parham, "it may seem amazing that the Pentecostal movement had managed to stay alive at all."[27] However, despite all appearances to the contrary, 10 percent of the world's population (which amounts to at least one-quarter of all Christians) since that time, and still today identify as falling within the Pentecostal or charismatic tradition. Therefore, in contemporary terms, we might say it seems that the movement

23. Parham, *The Everlasting Gospel*, 84.
24. Wacker, *Heaven Below*, 51.
25. Stephens, *The Fire Spreads*, 216.
26. Stephens, *The Fire Spreads*, 216.
27. MacArthur, "Tongue Tied," lines 26–29.

did not just manage to stay alive, but indeed thrived during the last century or so.[28]

THE DECLINING TONGUES PHENOMENON

Interestingly, despite the thriving statistical state of Pentecostalism, the phenomenon most often associated with the movement (i.e., speaking in tongues) is in a gradual but steady decline. Take, for example, a report published in 2013, by the *Associated Press*, titled "Messages in Tongues Down among Pentecostals." In this article, a journalist broke a story that featured on multiple news sites around the world, both secular and Christian. The article revealed details of AG officials being "worried about the decline in messages in tongues—or spirit baptism—at a general council meeting."[29] More worryingly for the broader Pentecostal movement, the article claimed that the practice of speaking in tongues had declined by at least 3 percent, the lowest total since 1995.[30] Following this report, another article, in *Christianity Today* in 2013, seemed to confirm the declension theory with an article titled, "Assemblies of God Leader Denies that Speaking in Tongues is in Decline." In their response, officials from the AG movement emphatically stated that in their view, reports on the decline of speaking in tongues were "totally inaccurate."[31] By way of contrast, however, in 2006, an article appeared in *Christianity Today* based on a Pew Research Center's survey suggested, "speaking in tongues . . . is not practiced by a significant number of Charismatic and Pentecostal Christians worldwide."[32]

Although there could be many reasons for the decline in speaking in tongues, clearly one reason stands out above all others. Essentially, some Pentecostals tend to shirk tongues-speaking

28. PEW Research Center, "Spirit and Power," lines 1–4.
29. Gryboski, "Assemblies of God Leader," lines 19–21.
30. Gryboski, "Assemblies of God Leader," lines 20–22.
31. Gryboski, "Assemblies of God Leader," line 6.
32. Banks, "Poll Says Many Pentecostals," lines 1–3.

The Pentecostal Paradox

altogether because of what they perceive to be a stigma attached to the practice. For example, according to commentator Harvey Cox, while speaking in tongues is a "long-developing phenomenon," there is a perception that those within the Pentecostal movement "don't want what appears to be objectionable to stick out or be viewed with suspicion."[33] Even so, according to the same *Christianity Today* article, many within Pentecostalism even think speaking in tongues is "not an appropriate modern-day practice, despite its use in biblical times."[34] There are other indications of a decline in the tongues phenomenon, which further research has supported. For example, studies show that almost half of those within the Pentecostal movement shirk the tongues phenomenon completely. A survey conducted by the Pew Research Center in 2006 found that of the six out of ten countries included in the study, some 40 percent of adherents to the Pentecostal faith claim that they never pray or speak in tongues.[35] A Spokesperson for the research group explained the following:

> I think that the classic Pentecostal belief that speaking in tongues was the real evidence of the second baptism of the Holy Spirit is, at least in practice, not widely accepted around the world.[36]

Even so, with the current data suggesting that speaking in tongues is in declension, the question remains, what effect will this loss have on the broader Pentecostal movement? Potentially, Pentecostal identity would be at risk by the loss of such a phenomenon. Of course, today, many Pentecostal groups most notably the AG, still hold that speaking in other tongues indicates the baptism in the Holy Spirit. For example, this organization requires all their ministers, annually, to sign documents asserting their belief that the initial evidence of having received the Spirit baptism is

---

33. Parvini, "Messages in Tongues Down," lines 18–20.
34. Banks, "Poll says Many Pentecostals," line 25.
35. Lugo and Green, "Pew Forum on Religion," lines 80–85.
36. Banks, "Poll Says Many Pentecostals," lines 14–18.

speaking in tongues.[37] This requirement, in a sense, aids in perpetuating the phenomenon throughout the AG movement. As a result, most of their pastors have to undertake a certain amount of "mental gymnastics" when it comes time to renew their ministerial credentials annually.[38] A useful illustration of this is the dilemma that arose when one of their founding members, FF Bosworth, in 1918, disagreed with this aspect of the AG constitution. Consequently, he handed in his credentials to the organization because of a disagreement over the tongues issue.[39] In essence, Bosworth believed that the insistence on the tongues phenomenon as evidence of having received the Spirit baptism, particularly by the AG movement, was essentially an erroneous belief. Accordingly, Bosworth wrote that Jesus "never taught this doctrine that all Spirit-baptized believers would speak in tongues. Then, why should we?"[40]

Further, Bosworth affirmed, "not one apostle, prophet, and not one of the greatest soul winners ever taught it, so it is clear that this doctrine is not essential to the greatest success."[41] However, it is unlikely that many AG ministers will follow Bosworth's example, anytime soon, for surveys show that most ministers within the AG movement are favorable to this clause. Besides, there are repercussions if any of their ministers disagree with this tenet. In addition, similar to Bosworth, refusal to comply would require the minister's resignation or, the revocation of their credentials.

So, will this practice change anytime soon? This seems unlikely, despite that fact; it is increasingly becoming something of controversial teaching among most Christians, but especially within the AG movement. Further, softening this stance on mandating speaking in tongues would risk sending the "AG traveling down a slippery slope of losing its Pentecostal identity and jeopardize the institutional well-being of this thriving denomination," writes

37. Assemblies of God, "The 57th Session."
38. Poloma and Green, *The Assemblies of God*, 84.
39. Friesen, *Norming the Abnormal*, 83–84.
40. Barnes, *F. F. Bosworth*, 104.
41. Barnes, *F. F. Bosworth*, 104.

Poloma.⁴² Indeed, it is this phenomenon above all else that defines its identity, so there are clear vested interests in maintaining the status quo. With this in mind, it seems that this mandated policy has caused a "small but growing number of pastors to question the biblical base for the doctrine" of speaking in tongues, explained Poloma.⁴³

As outlined above, not everyone in the Pentecostal movement adheres to the controversial tongues teaching. However, among the pastors of the AG movement, it is an entirely different story. Indeed, one study discovered that most ministers (some 85 percent) within the AG movement still affirmed the practice of speaking in tongues. In contrast, some 15 percent expressed elements of disagreement with the teaching.⁴⁴

THE SOUTHERN BAPTISTS' POSITION ON TONGUES

As a point of comparison, among the largest protestant denomination in the US, the Southern Baptists, the subject of speaking in tongues remains a contentious issue. For example, in an article titled "Tongues Survey Fuels Baptist Debate," a *Lifeway* research report revealed results, which are, if nothing else, interesting. In essence, the survey found that overall, half of Southern Baptist pastors believed in such a thing as a private prayer language.⁴⁵ Conversely, a disproportionate number of pastors within the Southern Baptist movement (some 41 percent) concluded that speaking in tongues ceased with the apostles of the early church.⁴⁶ Although the study is interesting, some within the Southern Baptist movement apparently have questioned the timing of the *Lifeway* Research. The main reason is that it occurred right before

---

42. Poloma, and Green, "The Assemblies of God," 84.
43. Poloma, and Green, "The Assemblies of God," 85.
44. Poloma, and Green, "The Assemblies of God," 84.
45. Lovelace, "Lifeway Releases Prayer," lines 32–44.
46. Lovelace, "Lifeway Releases Prayer," lines 32–44.

the meeting of the Southern Baptist Convention was due to be convened.

So, what is the Southern Baptists' official position on this issue today? According to a *Washington Post* report, "after a decade-long resistance, the Southern Baptist Convention will admit missionary candidates who speak in tongues." This practice, as the *Post* admitted, has long been "associated with Pentecostal and charismatic churches."[47] However, Pentecostal practices are slowly but surely infiltrating various areas of Christianity previously considered immune to Pentecostal ideology. Although on a calmer note, this change does not necessarily mean that the Southern Baptist movement will send out missionaries who actually speak in tongues anytime soon. However, "the practice would no longer lead to automatic disqualification," the organization further affirmed.[48]

BILLY GRAHAM'S VIEW ON SPEAKING IN TONGUES

Earlier, we mentioned the Southern Baptists' changing views on tongues so it might be useful to examine how their most famous son, Billy Graham, viewed this issue. While the late Graham was not known for taking a "bull in a China shop" approach on most issues, we will observe that he was more outspoken on the matter of speaking in tongues.

While many voices have made their position known on either side of this hotly debated Pentecostal issue, one person, Billy Graham, increasingly advocated a more middle-ground approach in the context of the baptism with the Holy Spirit. For example, speaking of the differences that divide us, Graham maintained that we should not shy away from stating specific differences of opinions. Yet, on the other hand, we should also at the same time attempt to understand one another's point of view and learn from and pray for each other. However, wrote Graham, when it comes to

---

47. Horton and Yonat, "Southern Baptists to Open," lines 1–2.
48. Horton and Yonat, "Southern Baptists to Open," lines 16–18.

"the question of the baptism with the Holy Spirit, in my judgment [this], is often more important than these other issues, especially when the doctrine of the baptism with the Spirit is distorted."[49] Interestingly, Graham further maintained that he has at times "wanted an experience." However, he wisely concluded that any experience must be Bible-based:

> It seems to me that we are baptized into the body of Christ by the Spirit at conversion. This is the only Spirit baptism . . . I do not see from scripture that this filling by the Holy Spirit constitutes a second baptism, nor do I see that speaking in tongues is a necessary accompaniment of being filled with the Spirit.[50]

Without question, there are varying opinions on the theory of the baptism in the Holy Spirit. Therefore, at the close of this chapter, based on the above data, a good question to ponder is whether the phenomenon of speaking in tongues is a necessary accompaniment in the life of the average Christian. In response, one author advocated a middle-ground approach, while simultaneously challenging the status quo among Pentecostals. In a book titled *How to be Pentecostal without Speaking in Tongues*, Tony Campolo made a searching statement. In this work (primarily for non-Pentecostals), he explained, "there is more to being a Christian than just believing the right doctrines and practicing the right rituals."[51]

Given the various interpretations of the tongues phenomenon advanced in this chapter, the jury is, as it were, still out on this issue. However, as this book ventures into the next chapter, it will ask whether it is necessary, or at all possible to go back to Pentecost, or not? Whether tongues were foreign languages, ecstatic utterances or otherwise, we may never know. Therefore, as Hoekema rightly concluded, "it seems difficult, if not impossible to make a final judgment on this matter."[52]

---

49. Graham, *The Collected Works*, 369.
50. Graham, *The Collected Works*, 369.
51. Campolo, *How to Be Pentecostal*, 2.
52. Hoekema, *What about Tongue Speaking?* 83.

6

Back to Pentecost! Or Not?

THE INAUGURAL EDITION OF the Azusa Street Mission's monthly magazine, *Apostolic Faith*, launched in September 1906, with much fanfare with the first edition of the magazine displaying a bold title stating, "A New Wave of Pentecost Has Come and Los Angeles Being Visited by a Revival of Bible Salvation and Pentecost as Recorded in the Book of Acts."[1] In a similar vein, the second issue's lead article triumphantly alerted its readers that the so-called promised latter rain is now being "poured out on God's humble people." Alarmingly, the article presented a "low view" of the historical gospel presented throughout the ages, with the claim that "only a partial gospel has been preached."[2] Further, the magazine triumphantly declared, "the Pentecostal baptism is being restored to the church." [3] Through, it would seem the early Pentecostal movement.

1. Seymour, *Apostolic Faith Magazine*.
2. Seymour, "Pentecostal Baptism Restored."
3. Seymour, "Pentecostal Baptism Restored."

THE EARLY HISTORY OF THE MOVEMENT

In trying to understand how Pentecostalism became the movement that it is today; this chapter will reach beyond the phenomenon and view this movement from a broader historical context. Historically, even though the term Pentecostal is better known today, initially a different title described Pentecostalism from its earliest times, namely the Apostolic Faith Mission. This reflected, in part, at least the idea of returning to an earlier period of church history. The "new Pentecost," as they termed it, was in a sense viewed by the movement as the re-entry of Pentecostalism in modern-day history; it had leaped over the intervening years, returning the church to an era that followed the same "way the apostles trod."[4] In doing so, they believed they were returning to the days of the early church in their search for authentic faith and practice. This 2,000-year leap of church history, however, is a foreign concept throughout the ages of the church, leading up to the turn of the twentieth century before the rise of Pentecostalism.

The dawning of a new era was, in part, the reason that so many in the Pentecostal movement continues to believe they were living the last days. In fact, as will be apparent shortly, there were no precedents for Pentecostalism before the turn of the twentieth century. This turn-of-the-century event marked a time when the movement developed its emphasis on returning to Pentecost, along with all the supernatural phenomena associated with such a claim. Much of the Pentecostal literature, especially from the earlier years, abounds with implications of "last days' ministry" and the sense that "time is growing short," or that Christ's return will be "very, very soon."[5] Even to this day, the practice of Pentecostalism still proceeds with an inherent, end-time mission theology.[6] Indeed, it seems that the need to reignite the flame of a bygone era became an active part of the focus of Pentecostal teaching throughout its tenure. If anything, this represents a marked shift,

   4. French, *Early Interracial Oneness*, 10.
   5. See McClung, *Historical Perspectives*, 46.
   6. See McClung, *Historical Perspectives*, 46.

not only among the Pentecostals but also in the history of the church. A typical example of this shift is observable in the efforts made to corroborate the events of the history of the church, to match the Pentecostal belief of a new day dawning at the turn of the twentieth century. For the most part, within Pentecostalism, the often-stated aim was that of a return to the early church period, in essence, if not in actuality. Ultimately, this concept was and still is to a certain extent, an integral part of the thinking within the Pentecostal movement worldwide.

This desire to return to Pentecost is a concept that is by definition difficult, if not unachievable. For what occurred on the day of Pentecost (from where Pentecostals derive their name) was, in essence, a unique, non-repeatable outpouring of the Spirit.[7] Therefore, as Kuyper rightly stated, "to pray for another outpouring or Baptism in the Holy Spirit is not correct and empty of any real meaning," and would, in effect, "deny the Pentecost miracle."[8] Pentecostalism is set apart by its structure; it only emerged on the world scene at the beginning of the twentieth century. Before this time, the movement had no history, yet at the same time, the Pentecostal movement claims to have leaped all the intervening years (i.e., 2,000 years of church history), with the recurrent theme of going "back to Pentecost."[9]

In support of this claim, of the reemergence of Pentecostal practice, early Pentecostals did one of two things. On the one hand, they either disregarded the entire history of the church, citing the church's plunge into the Dark Ages with the light barely flickering during those times. Or else they sought to establish a restoration motif, which stated that although tongues-speaking all but disappeared during the apostolic age, it miraculously reappeared during the Azusa Street Mission revival in 1906.

---

7. Grenz, *Theology for the Community of God*, 419.
8. Kuyper, *The Work of the Holy Spirit*, 127.
9. See Lawrence, *Three Early Pentecostal Tracts*, 12.

THE PENTECOSTAL PARADOX

BACK TO PENTECOST! OR NOT?

Back to Pentecost! How significant is this cry and is it at all necessary that Christians in the twenty-first century should go back 2,000 years to what occurred on the day of Pentecost? It is a good question; undoubtedly, we can find inspiration in that history. However, is it necessary? Second, should we use this as a pattern or paradigm on which to model the Christian experience of our day?[10]

The purpose of this chapter is to explore the Pentecostal claim of a restored church. There is a belief within Pentecostal circles that the movement has literally "leaped" off the pages of the Bible. In a sense, in Pentecostals' eyes, this fosters the idea of a return to the New Testament era. It claims, "Bible days are here again," and the events of the Azusa Street Mission were the day of Pentecost revisited.[11] Therefore, this belief has persisted that tongues-speaking and miracle-working, having all but disappeared during the apostolic age, re-emerged through their instrumentality in the twentieth century.[12] However, this raises some valid questions such as how something that is seemingly so rare throughout church history becomes a necessary element of our daily faith and practice?[13] Indeed, replete among the literature in modern Pentecostalism is an underlying nuance that, "God has raised us up."[14] This engenders a feeling of identification with the early church in the book of Acts. In a sense, it lends itself to the particular idea that through Pentecostalism, God has restored apostolic Christianity.[15]

To comprehend the meaning of these earlier claims of Pentecostal phenomena being restored, it may be helpful to ask some questions. For example, what actually occurred in the intervening

---

10. See Gladden, "Back to Pentecost," 203.
11. See Dempster, *Pacifism in Pentecostalism*, 144.
12. Weaver, *New Apostolic Reformation*, 22.
13. See Dayton, "The Limits of Evangelicalism," 45.
14. See McClung, *Truth on Fire*, 82–90.
15. See Dayton, "The Limits of Evangelicalism," 45.

period before the Pentecostal movement debuted on the world scene? It is clear that God has been at work in the period leading up to the Pentecostal movement becoming prominent. To say otherwise would be a false assumption. In essence, it would be like saying that the wind has not blown in over 2,000 years![16]

Nevertheless, if we have no recourse to the thoughts on this issue, of those who have gone before us, what are we left with? We are left to figure out for ourselves what happened in the intervening years leading up to and beyond the launch of the Pentecostal movement of 1906. It is one thing to claim that as a church we are returning to Pentecost. It is, however, quite another to actually know what occurred during those silent years as the church turned the corner into the centuries of the early church's establishment. During this time, there was, according to some Pentecostal writers, a temporary cessation of the Spirit's dynamic activity.[17] Others see an unbroken line of succession from Pentecost to the present. This thought, however, is hard to prove and may not find credence throughout church history. Pentecostal author Liardon believes that this so-called "temporary cessation, of the gifts and the miraculous was not the result of the stopping of a dispensation time clock."[18] According to this view, it was a direct result of the church "having lost touch of the dimensions of the other realm."[19] For this reason, the question that naturally arises is whether this so-called "dispensation time clock" has actually ticked once again? If it has, this will prove a continuation point of view. However, there is no easy way to confirm the claim of restored Pentecostal phenomena throughout the twentieth and into the twenty-first centuries, without first delving into the history of the church to gauge understanding on this matter. There is a serious lack of evidence throughout the last 2,000 years of church history of Pentecostal-type phenomena even having occurred. Even so, in the eyes of the classical Pentecostal, there were still supposedly "pockets of

16. Oliver, *Pentecost to the Present*, xvi.
17. Liardon, *The Azusa Street Revival*, 18.
18. Liardon, *The Azusa Street Revival*, 18.
19. Liardon, *The Azusa Street Revival*, 18.

The Pentecostal Paradox

Pentecostals" in existence before the movement became prominent.[20] If that is the case, and the so-called "dispensational" clock is ticking once again, a 2,000-year leap of church history certainly could be justified. Therefore, it would be helpful at this stage to gauge the consensus of the early church fathers throughout the years leading to the Pentecostal leap.

Pentecostal historian Anderson, in *An Introduction to Pentecostalism*, mused that the "Church Fathers never suggested that any of the gifts of the Spirit had ceased."[21] However, to gauge the ramifications of this assertion, it might be useful here to take a closer look at what the early church had to say on this matter. This will become the focus of the rest of the chapter.

While not all early church fathers (i.e., before Pentecostalism) were correct all the time, difficulties begin to emerge when we sideline their opinions. After all, they have been what Newman called, "guardians of the gospel" throughout the ages; therefore, it is in our interest to respect their opinions.[22] Accordingly, in the words of Hunter, "the prestige of the fathers demands that attention be paid to their assessment of any doctrine that claims to be biblical."[23] In addition to this, as will be apparent shortly, the oldest interpretation, the one that is most accepted in church history, understood that tongues-speaking in the first church were intelligible foreign languages (i.e., native languages; see chapter 5).[24] Moody echoed this sentiment, stating that although, "speaking in tongues has been interpreted in many ways . . . the church fathers are almost unanimous on foreign languages."[25] It is interesting to note that Irenaeus, perhaps the closest to the apostolic times, a pupil of Polycarp (who was a disciple of John the Apostle), spoke of those "who possess prophetic gifts and who through the spirit speak all kinds of languages and bring to light for the general

---

20. Liardon, *The Azusa Street Revival*, 19.
21. Anderson, *An Introduction to Pentecostalism*, 20.
22. Newman, *The Ultimate Evidence*, xiv.
23. Hunter, *Spirit Baptism*, 122.
24. Garrett, *Systematic Theology*, 227.
25. Moody, *Spirit of the Living God*, 62.

benefit the hidden things."²⁶ However, despite this statement, between the periods of the book of Acts and Irenaeus, there is little evidence to suggest that any Christians experienced firsthand incidents in which they could speak in a language they had not learned. Indeed, if that were the case, it would be expected that the Pentecostal experience would have become wider spread. As a result, there would have been at least some traces in the writings of the early Christians that indicated such an experience.²⁷

As outlined in chapter 5, according to early Pentecostal thought, Christians could enter foreign missionary fields with little or no local linguistics. They thought that like the first apostles before them, they too could communicate in a native language without prior learning. Despite their best efforts, they soon realized that this was not the case. From this experience, they toggled the meaning of tongues, and from then on, speaking in tongues took on an entirely new meaning. Rather than the unlearned ability to speak a foreign language, it became an unintelligible prayer language. Ironically, this decision, which is now a staple in Pentecostal circles, arose from the futile and failed attempts at missionary work.

In more recent history, Stedman recognized this truth, stating, "there is no New Testament record of the private use of tongues . . . the biblical gift of tongues was everywhere publicly exercised and was evidently not intended for private use."²⁸ Besides, there is no sign in later church history of any continuance of the gifts carried over from the early church to the present. In fact, the only mention of tongues in the Bible, outside the book of Acts, was in the letters to the Corinthian Church. Evidently, after this time, the tongues issue fell into disdain and neglect, so much so that the gift has carried little or no significance since that time. The biblical record discourages both the cultivation and use of tongues; the Bible clearly states in First Corinthians 14:19, it is better to speak five words that are understood than "than ten thousand words in a tongue."

26. Saint Irenaeus, *The Writings of Irenaeus*, 68.
27. Mills, *Speaking in Tongues*, 87.
28. Stedman, *Body Life*, 46.

[29] What was the gift of tongues on the day of Pentecost? We may never know; however, one thing here is clear—the attitude toward this matter "is certainly not an encouragement for the continuance of the gift. This is especially so, given that there is ample evidence that often little or no change occurred in any of those who experienced it."[30] So, the next question is where did the present-day Pentecostal movement practice of tongues emanate from? After all, it almost disappeared without a trace in the vast history of the church. It seems that from around the time of Chrysostom to the Reformation, those "manifestations which had been so prominent in the early church," i.e., the charismatic gifts, especially speaking in tongues, seem to have all but disappeared—almost entirely—explained historian Nichol.[31] One of the clearest and perhaps most notable references about whether the tongues phenomenon continued uninterrupted throughout the church comes from the writings of the renowned Chrysostom. In his writings, this early church leader made it clear that the gift of tongues has ceased long before his time. He lived around 344–407. In his commentary on Corinthians, he admitted that these matters were "very obscure: but the obscurity is produced by our ignorance of the facts referred to and by their cessation, being such as then used to occur, but now no longer take place."[32] That is quite a statement and outlines the position of the early church on this matter. Similarly, Augustine (354–430) echoed this sentiment, explaining that tongues were these signs adapted to the time "that thing was done for a betokening [sign], and it passed away"[33] Following on from the views of Augustine, Martin Luther, for example, was adamant that tongues should be coupled with interpretation if they are used at all. Ultimately, however, Luther believed that speaking in tongues should only be permitted "if at the same time it is interpreted," so

29. NKJV.
30. See Gladden, "Back to Pentecost," 206–210.
31. Nichol, *Pentecostalism*, 21.
32. Chrysostom, *Homilies of Saint John*, 395.
33. Augustine, *Homilies on the Gospel*, 1172.

that one can understand it.³⁴ This view, although a slight departure from most of the church fathers is still vastly different from many of the views that are taught today on this matter. As such, if Luther's view is correct, this cuts across the claim of speaking in tongues as being a restored prayer language. Another reformer worth noting is John Calvin, who also did not witness tongues and other such phenomena in his day. Calvin believed that the apostles received what he called "distinctive tongues." Why? Well, according to this line of reasoning, it equipped the early church "that they might spread that abroad amongst all people which was delivered to them."³⁵ Note the term used in the above statement: "distinctive tongues." Compare this with the current claim of experiencing the phenomenon of devotional tongues. What is this term, "devotional tongues," and is it a valid experience? Well, this aspect of the tongues phenomenon in Pentecostal parlance is, according to this view, "sometimes called a prayer language." ³⁶ However, if it is a valid experience, it certainly is obscure given that those who practice the phenomenon are apparently unaware of what they are saying. Also, those who hear it are also none the wiser. However, as before stated by Chrysostom, any obscurity is only caused by our "ignorance of the facts."³⁷

So, does the phenomenon of speaking in tongues belong to our day? An appropriate answer to this question comes from John Calvin. He stated that tongues "does not properly attain to us, for because Christ meant to set forth the beginning of his kingdom with these miracles."³⁸ Further to this, the Reformer explained, "although we do not receive it, that we may speak with tongues that we may be prophets, that we may cure the sick, that we may work miracles; yet it was given to us for a better use that we may believe with the heart."³⁹ Clearly, Calvin's belief, which was shared by

34. Stjerna, *The Annotated Luther*, 100.
35. Calvin, *The Acts of the Apostles*, 75.
36. Assemblies of God, "Baptism in the Holy Spirit," lines 300–320.
37. See Gladden, "Back to Pentecost," 206.
38. Calvin *The Acts of the Apostles*, 158, 121.
39. Calvin, *Commentary on The Acts of the Apostles*, 121.

The Pentecostal Paradox

many within the early church—was that tongues were suited for a time and specific purpose—to enable the early church to proclaim the message that had been "delivered to them."[40] In a similar vein, Torrey (see chapter 8), believed that throughout the ages, the gift of language was evidently so misused among the Corinthians to whom Paul wrote that it was no longer relevant to the church. Another reason given for the ceasing of the miraculous gifts, especially tongues, was that they "failed or ceased because they were of little value to the religious community."[41] Clearly, given that there is scant mention throughout the Bible, it would appear this phenomenon is of little value to God as well! Interestingly, the writer of most of the New Testament, the apostle Paul, never once directed the Corinthians to whom he wrote to seek tongues. In fact, speaking in tongues, as before mentioned is never mentioned in any book of the Bible outside the letter to the Corinthian Church. In this case, according to Flynn, the writer "soft-pedals it and tries to correct its abuses."[42]

SUMMARY

According to Chrysostom, such gifts, although they "used to occur," no longer take place.[43] Augustine stated that tongues were a sign adapted to the time and "that thing was done for a betokening [sign] and passed away."[44]

Calvin explained that speaking with tongues lasted only for a time. It seems that from the above statements, there is but one recurring theme throughout the history of the church. That is, that such gifts served their purpose, lasting but for a time and then passing away.

---

40. Calvin, *Commentary on The Acts of the Apostles*, 75.
41. Scott, *What Happened at Pentecost*, 153.
42. Flynn, *19 Gifts of the Spirit*, 209.
43. Chrysostom, *Homilies of Saint John*, 395.
44. Saint Augustine, *Homilies on the Gospel*, 1172.

IS IT NECESSARY TO RETURN TO PENTECOST?

The problem with this approach—as Stanford reminded us—is that when the Pentecostal movement discusses going back to Pentecost; they actually, do not go back far enough.[45] In our desire for the miraculous, we often forget that before Pentecost was the "death, resurrection, and ascension of Jesus Christ." Perhaps most importantly, Stanford noted that the message of the gospel ought to be the focus and not the "modern theatrics" of the events of Pentecost.[46]

The absolute standard, then, as Newman correctly stated, is the word of God, which is the only basis for any catalytic point of discussion.[47] This is a recognized principle, which has been honored by the guardians of the gospel from the days of the Reformers. We must acknowledge it in our day as well. However, we should always be open to adjust or reform our thinking, especially when we are challenged in the light of a "fuller and more competent understanding of the word of God."[48]

Therefore, here we are, over a century later, and we find that tongues, visions, and prophecies are indicative of a sign of God's blessing. If this is the case, as is so ardently believed among those of the Pentecostal tradition, as sad as it is, Mormonism actually purports to have the same phenomenon in their teaching. For example, consider the writings of Lucy Smith, the mother of Joseph Smith (the founder of Mormonism). Alarmingly, in her journal, she stated that her sons all assembled in what they called the "school of the prophets." They then all "spoke in tongues and prophesied."[49] Therefore, activities such as speaking in tongues and prophecy are not limited to charismatic-type phenomena. The danger here is that when we raise our experiences to the point of a maxim, we tread on dangerous ground. It is best to follow the

---

45. Stanford, *The Pentecostal Takeover*, 77.
46. Stanford, *The Pentecostal Takeover*, 77.
47. Newman, *The Ultimate Evidence*, xiv.
48. Newman, *The Ultimate Evidence*, xiv.
49. Smith, Biographical *Sketches* 197.

beliefs that have endured throughout the history of the church and not create a standard out of new teaching that is not endorsed by myriads that have handed down their beliefs to the contrary.

7

The Mishaps of the Movement

OVER THE LAST CENTURY, the Pentecostal movement has gone on from strength-to-strength. Remarkably, from a core membership (as mentioned in chapter 1) of just 50 or 60 members in 1906, it has now become a global phenomenon. In fact, it has grown so significantly that by 1970; it counted around 67 million adherents.[1] The logistics of this type of growth are momentous when one considers that this figure represents a staggering million-fold increase. Since then, the movement has enjoyed another tenfold increase, bringing it to just less than 670 million heading into the twenty-first century.[2] Whether these are inflated figures, over-optimistic, or even miscalculated, as some would suggest, this growth represents a considerable part of the Christian church.[3] However, this kind of growth did not come about without difficulties that all but threatened the very existence of Pentecostalism altogether. To this end, the rest of the chapter will explore the mishaps of the movement.

Initially, the Pentecostal movement undoubtedly made great strides. However, this astonishing pace did not last long. After

1. Anderson, *To the Ends of the Earth*, 248.
2. Johnson et al., "Christianity 2017," 41–52.
3. See Ziefle, *The Charismatic Renewal*, 123.

The Pentecostal Paradox

several euphoric years, they soon faced difficulties that would threaten to tear the movement apart. In the end, problems emerged not only from outside Pentecostalism but also from within its own ranks.[4]

It was Azusa Street, where Pentecostalism first constructed its various networks that would eventually define the movement. Being Pentecostalism's epicenter—one would expect to find unity there—yet, any agreement that existed would ultimately be dissolved. Soon, much of the Azusa Street Mission scene faced fragmentation.[5] At one point, this unity was indeed a reality there. But surprisingly, despite repeated declarations of Christian unity, according to Blumhofer, some of those within the early Pentecostal movement bickered constantly among themselves.[6]

The term "fragmentation" would almost automatically suggest rancor and divisions; however, Jacobson contended, "those enemies of unity are very hard to find. Most early Pentecostal leaders were committed to Christian unity."[7] Contrary to the above statement, as this chapter will show, evidence exists that there were disruptions to the original unity of the movement.

PERSONAL DIFFICULTIES EMERGE

Indeed, all newly formed organizations have their share of controversies, and the early Pentecostals were not immune to this. And we find things took a turn for the worse, with most of the deterioration beginning to set in between 1907 and 1908. Therefore, just over one year from the initial launch of the Azusa Street Mission, the fragmentation process began. At this time, several key staff members actively involved in the new Pentecostal work parted ways with Seymour. One of these, Florence Crawford, disagreed with Seymour's marriage to parishioner Jenny Moore in 1908. As

---

4. Synan, *The Holiness-Pentecostal Tradition*, 149.
5. Jacobson, *Thinking in the Spirit*, 10.
6. Blumhofer, *Restoring the Faith*, 125.
7. Jacobson, *Thinking in the Spirit*, 10.

The Mishaps of the Movement

a result, Crawford, along with another prominent female member Clara Lum, also left the movement heading to Portland, Oregon.[8] In doing so, they severed the fledgling Azusa Street Mission's only link to the broader world. The mailing lists of the monthly periodical, *Apostolic Faith*, mysteriously disappeared. This magazine had become a beacon of the new Pentecostal movement, which at the time could boast over 50,000 monthly subscribers. However, through an extraordinary turn of events, the new hub of the magazine—at least from an administrative perspective—now resided in Portland, Oregon.

The mailing list disappearance could not have come at a worse time for Seymour and the new Pentecostal movement. The rapid speed with which things had declined was startling. Most historians agree that the perpetrators were the two disgruntled employees/volunteers mentioned earlier. Indeed, Lum appeared to be the driving force behind the *Apostolic Faith* magazine. She worked tirelessly for many years as a stenographer and editor for the Azusa Street Mission. Consequently, Lum recorded many of the events of the Mission's work.[9] As an assistant, Crawford co-edited the magazine and was generally a helper in the movement.[10]

The magazine's large circulation is cited as one reason for the initial growth of the Pentecostal movement. Therefore, it was not long before the loss of the publication contributed to the slow demise of the Los Angeles base.[11] The loss of subscribers and the editorial staff eventually crippled the movement, which ultimately brought about the purported failure of the work at the Azusa Street Mission.[12]

After the mailing list debacle, Seymour became frantic. He embarked upon a hasty trip to Portland, Oregon, to attempt their recovery. However, this was to no avail. Disheartened, he returned

---

8. Synan and Fox, *William J. Seymour*, 351.
9. Robeck, *The Azusa Street Mission*, 305.
10. Robinson, *Divine Healing*, 27.
11. King, *The Bible in History*, 262.
12. Robinson, *Divine Healing*, 27.

to the headquarters of the Azusa Street Mission, minus the mailing list.

Given that these splits and factions occurred just after the mailing list saga, there is every reason to believe that the marriage of Seymour and Moore was the catalyst that tore the movement apart. This spontaneous marriage, held as a private ceremony, sadly, caused unnecessary rifts and contentions all within just a couple of years of the launch of the Azusa Street Mission.[13] The reason for this parting of ways remains open to debate among scholars, and the precise reasons may never be known. However, one aspect too clear to overlook is that Crawford was the one who took the initiative and broke her relationship with Seymour. However, it seems that a private motive on Lum's part may well have added fuel to the already simmering flames.

Some contend that Lum may have felt betrayed when Seymour married Moore in light of their close relationship. Therefore, wrote Barfoot, "whether jilted or not, Clara Lum turned to Florence Crawford for solace and support." And more than anything else, it seems that Florence Crawford was the one who was "dead set" against the important institution of marriage.[14]

As mentioned in chapter 2, in the early years of its establishment, apocalyptic fervor, it seems, was a driving force of the Pentecostal movement. Lum, like many others, mistakenly viewed marriage, "as a step that undermined the strongly held doctrine of the imminence of the Second Coming."[15]

In sharp contrast to this unusual view of marriage, which appears to have prevailed at the time, Seymour took quite a different perspective; indeed, he tried to correct this misconstrued notion about marriage by publishing several extracts promoting this God-ordained institution. Seymour, for his part, was adamant that marriage was an honorable act. To this end, he instructed that

---

13. Robinson, *Divine Healing*, 27.
14. Barfoot, *Aimee Semple McPherson*, 141.
15. Robinson, *Divine Healing*, 27.

The Mishaps of the Movement

to forbid it on the grounds of religious belief was the doctrine of devils.[16]

Not long after this break with the Azusa Street Mission, Crawford formed an independent work in Portland, Oregon. To the dismay of many within the movement, Crawford even used the same name for this new movement, which originated with Parham: the Apostolic Faith Movement. Indeed, the departure of the two valuable workers, Crawford and Lum, struck a harsh blow to the leadership of Seymour and by extension, the entire Pentecostal movement along the Pacific coast.[17]

Besides these problems, new difficulties would emerge. Indeed, these would cause even more significant disruptions than the movement had ever faced as the work suffered, not only from internal disputes but from threats from other quarters as well. In describing these emerging problems, Pentecostal historian Liardon explained that three key events led to the Azusa Street Mission's disintegration. These were racism, doctrinal controversy, and personal strife.[18] Having already examined the personal strife issue, we can now focus on the next emerging difficulty, which emerged from within the Mission's ranks.

DOCTRINAL DIFFICULTIES DEVELOP

At one point, things seemed to settle a little after the early difficulties. However, it had not been long before the calmer atmosphere within the Azusa Street Mission was undermined. An enigmatic figure would emerge from the shadows who would loom large on the Pentecostal scene and have repercussions within much of Christendom as well. William Durham (1873–1912) was something of a divisive type, who became interim pastor at the Azusa Street Mission while Seymour was away ministering throughout the East Coast of the US. Surprisingly, Seymour's wife Jenny

---

16. Liardon, *The Azusa Street Revival*, 164
17. Robeck, *The Azusa Street Mission*, 300
18. Liardon, *The Azusa Street Revival*, 189.

The Pentecostal Paradox

invited Durham to speak at the Azusa Street Mission in her husband's absence.[19] Unbeknownst, however, to Seymour, Durham was amassing quite a following. At this time, Durham preached what Pentecostal author Espinosa called, "another gospel."[20] So, what was this other gospel and what effect did it have on the broader Pentecostal movement? In essence, this new teaching—called the Finished Work—deemed the three-stage post-conversion experience, which in Pentecostal circles they often term the Second Blessing, as essentially invalid. Typically, these so-called "extra blessings" were an adjunct to an initial conversion experience. This created a three-stage process. This second experience, according to a Pentecostal tradition, maintained that it was possible to attain a state of supposed Christian perfection in this life. As a result, most Pentecostals today, hold that there are only two so-called blessings (e.g., the conversion experience and then the Spirit baptism or speaking in tongues).

Not long after Durham's arrival, he persuaded thousands of Pentecostals to abandon their ideas about any second work of grace. Essentially, the outcome of this newest contagion polarized Pentecostals into two different camps.[21] This new teaching soon became so popular that by 1936; most Pentecostal movements globally had adopted this view.[22]

Even though both Parham and Seymour rejected Durham's Finished Work message; ironically, the AG picked it up and today, this two-stage "total package" version of Pentecostalism forms an integral part of their official teaching.[23] Therefore, it can indeed be said that Durham altered not only the beliefs of Pentecostalism but much of Christendom as well.

The setbacks of the earlier years eventually took their toll on the atmosphere at the Azusa Street Mission. After the arrival of W. B. Godbey (see chapter 8), the atmosphere at the Azusa Street

19. Alexander, *Black Fire*, 150.
20. See Espinosa, "Ordinary Prophet," 53.
21. King, *The Bible in History*, 262.
22. Stephens, *The Fire Spreads*, 237.
23. Pugh, *Bold Faith*, 5–6.

The Mishaps of the Movement

Mission was still nothing short of electric. Indeed, Godbey reported that Los Angeles was on tiptoe with expectancy when he arrived in the city in 1909.[24] Conversely, by Durham's arrival in Los Angeles on February 12, 1911, he described the Pentecostal work of the Azusa Street Mission as being in "total disarray." Apparently, the church comprised "only about a dozen" members, mainly African Americans, which made up the total number at this time.[25] However, this would soon change upon Durham's arrival at the Azusa Street Mission. Once again, the crowds returned, thronging the Azusa Street venue, practically emptying the other Pentecostal churches in the city.[26] Not long after this event, "the fire began to fall again at old Azusa as at the beginning," Bartleman later stated.[27]

Although it appeared that Durham's arrival had brought a much-needed revival, it only had the effect of sharply dividing the movement into two camps. Those who followed Durham rejected the then-current Pentecostal teaching of the second and third blessings, insisting there were but two works of grace, calling any third work a "fictitious experience." Those of the older Pentecostal tradition believed that Scripture did in effect, not support removing the third work of grace. As a result, they felt this new teaching would undermine the very foundations that the Pentecostal movement held dear.[28]

In reality, one reason that the Durham debacle even occurred was a belief that Seymour was not capable of leading the Azusa Street Mission anymore.[29] Taking advantage of this impasse, Durham lobbied to control the Azusa Street Mission. This prompted an early return by Seymour, and an unpleasant confrontation ensued.[30]

24. Godbey, "Tongue Movement Satanic," 4.
25. Robeck, *The Azusa Street Mission*, 316.
26. Menzies, *Anointed to Serve*, 76.
27. Bartleman, *Azusa Street*, 118.
28. Synan, *The Holiness-Pentecostal Tradition*, 151.
29. See Robeck, Seymour, William Joseph, 1056–1057.
30. See Robeck, Seymour, William Joseph, 1053–1057.

THE PENTECOSTAL PARADOX

To make matters worse, on Sunday, April 30, Durham said, "let us put it to a vote," asking for a "show of hands" as to who would side with Seymour or follow Durham.[31] The vote was decisive in favor of the latter. By this time, tempers were near boiling point. Seymour, hearing rumors of the attempted takeover, returned immediately from the East Coast to face Durham in the early part of May 1911.[32]

Indeed, it is easy to imagine Seymour's surprise to find Durham preaching contrary to his long-held beliefs. Meanwhile, while trying to avoid a confrontation, Seymour locked the doors against Durham. Unbeknown to them, however, they had supposedly "locked God and the saints out also from the old cradle of power."[33] Soon after this, Durham relocated to another part of town to continue his meetings. Once again, the crowds thronged the meeting house. Bartleman (who at this stage had deserted Seymour), stated, "the Lord was with Durham in great power," so much so that the Azusa Street Mission had, by 1912, become all but deserted.[34]

Durham's demise was swift and sudden. It was not long before he grew ill. In a strange turn of events, six months before Durham's death in early 1912, Parham took the grandstand once again, announcing to the world that the Finished Work issue would once and for all be settled. He contended that God would decisively intervene by removing the wrong teacher. Sadly, on July 7, 1912, Durham passed away at only 39 years of age.

Parham felt vindicated, as he declared, "how signally God has answered."[35] However, any satisfaction for Parham was relatively short-lived, as at least two-thirds of Pentecostals had left the Azusa Street Mission to follow Durham. Borlase explained, "the three-staged approach would never last. Instead, it was Durham's concept of the power of the cross that would become the default setting for

31. Robeck, *The Azusa Street Mission and Revival*, 317.
32. Borlase, *William Seymour: A Biography*, 215.
33. Bartleman, *Azusa Street*, 118.
34. Bartleman, *Azusa Street*, 118.
35. Blumhofer, *Restoring the Faith*, 125.

the modern Pentecostal movement."[36] From this point, the Pentecostal movement in Los Angeles became "hopelessly divided."[37] In addition, Durham had persuaded thousands of Pentecostals to abandon their ideas about any third work of grace.

Another issue to emerge was the oneness controversy, which arose in 1913. This teaching marked a pronounced shift in the history of Pentecostalism. At this time, many departed from the teaching so prominent in the Bible of God revealed in three persons (commonly called the Trinity). Indeed, these difficulties only worsened for the early Pentecostals, with Bartleman—the foremost chronicler of the movement (who earlier declared that the "color line was washed away by the blood of Christ")[38] eventually succumbing to the so-called oneness teaching.[39] This oneness formula, although broadly rejected by most Pentecostals at one stage, became endemic within the Pentecostal movement. For example, in 1916, as many as one-quarter of AG ministers left to join the oneness movement.[40] This divisive teaching nullified the person of Christ, three entities expressed in one being. Thomas Fudge perhaps sums this view up best in a book titled *Christianity without a Cross*.[41]

DISCRIMINATION DIFFICULTIES DEVELOP

Having examined the personal difficulties and doctrinal issues, the next problem that Pentecostalism faced, ironically, was racial discrimination. Sadly, a movement that was once renowned for its inclusiveness began once again to find that divisions were brewing within its ranks. Members turned against one another. It was not long before the inclusiveness had receded with the multiplying

36. Borlase, *William Seymour*, 217.
37. See Espinosa, "Ordinary Prophet," 54.
38. Liardon, *The Azusa Street Revival*, 104.
39. French, *Early Interracial Oneness*, 54.
40. Maseko, *Church Schism*, 568.
41. Fudge, *Christianity without the Cross*.

The Pentecostal Paradox

conflicts, especially between 1913 and 1917. By this time, explained Espinosa, what little flame was remaining within the movement was "just about snuffed out"[42] As a result, the interracial harmony that so defined the Azusa Street Mission eventually succumbed to the "popular racism of the time."[43]

After facing so many divisions, Seymour's overarching concerns now had become more pressing, as personal issues became a priority. From here, Seymour aimed to concentrate on combatting fanaticism and dogmatic beliefs. Stating his position even more firmly, he wrote that "some whites, like Parham, not only divided the Azusa Street Mission but also brought in a divisive and fanatical spirit by being too dogmatic in their insistence that speaking in tongues was the only physical evidence of the baptism with the Holy Spirit."[44] As a result, this led him to make the historic decision to reject Parham's original theory that speaking in tongues was the evidence of Spirit baptism.[45]

Another blow came as the early Pentecostals became institutionalized. Initially, when describing the unification of the movement, Pentecostal historian Nichol coined the term "undenominationalism."[46] Well, this phrase described the initial inclusiveness of the Azusa Street Mission. In fact, similar to many other developing movements, before long, the early Pentecostals did not view themselves as a separate entity. Rather, "they thought of themselves as a movement within the Christian Church, used by God to revitalize it."[47] Inevitably, the Azusa Street Mission eventually organized. Bartleman in effect wrote, "Azusa Street began to fail the Lord early in her history."[48]

In a strange turn of events, Bartleman stood up in one of the Azusa Street meetings, warning members against forming separate

42. See Espinosa, "Ordinary Prophet," 55.
43. Roberts, *African American Christian Ethics*, 172.
44. See Espinosa, "Ordinary Prophet," 56.
45. See Espinosa, "Ordinary Prophet," 56.
46. Nichol, *Pentecostalism*, 56.
47. Holland, *The Religious Dimension*, 338.
48. Davenport, *Azusa Revisited*, 283.

The Mishaps of the Movement

denominations. Soon after issuing this stark warning, Bartleman, as if vindicated, wrote, "sure enough after I had spoken this warning in the meeting, I found a sign outside the building, which read the Apostolic Faith Mission."[49] From then, this was the new name for the Azusa Street Mission. All this is a reminder of the Pentecostal movement's stated aim of wanting to revert to the times of the early church.

Allegiances are fickle and surprisingly, Bartleman himself—in August 1906—began another church only several blocks away from Azusa Street on the corner of Eighth and Maple Street. Adamantly, he asserted, "the atmosphere at Eighth and Maple was for a time, even deeper than at Azusa Street."[50]

Initially, racial inclusiveness was the order of the day within the Azusa Street Mission. However, new conflicts soon rose to the surface. In 1915, just nine years after the movement's formation, further rivalries would again develop between several leaders. In part, this led to the landmark decision by Seymour to change certain aspects of the Azusa Street Mission's constitution. The new declaration allowed only "people of color" to serve on the board of trustees and as bishops.[51] Further, Seymour sought to make sure that his successor would be a person of color.[52]

Although this would not always be a hard and fast rule, as there were occasional exceptions, this though would be later in the movement's development.

In attempting to uphold this new rule, in 1915, the Azusa Street Mission published several revised articles within its constitution. Eventually, this enabled Seymour to become bishop of the entire "Pacific Faith Movement."[53] It seems; however, this unusual step ostensibly was due more to the controversies that had risen within the movement than it was an issue of pure racism as such. Accordingly, Montier stated, "prejudice and dissension had

49. Davenport, *Azusa Revisited*, 283.
50. Davenport, *Azusa Revisited*, 285.
51. See Espinosa, "Ordinary Prophet," 56.
52. See Espinosa, "Ordinary Prophet," 67.
53. Montier, *Remembering the Past*, 11.

The Pentecostal Paradox

surfaced, and Bishop Seymour wanted to make sure that blacks had a prominent place in leadership positions."[54] This, however, clearly shows that tensions were present early in the movement.

We have observed in this chapter through the obstacles and opposition that the Pentecostal movement faced things changed over time and as a result, inner skirmish profoundly affected the broader Pentecostal movement. In the next chapter, the focus shifts to one of the most challenging parts of this book for the author to write titled Azusa Street and its Antagonists. This chapter will detail the views of several prominent eyewitnesses who were privy to firsthand knowledge of the Azusa Street Mission events as they happened.

---

54. Montier, *Remembering the Past*, 11.

8

Azusa Street and its Antagonists

ONE OF THE MOST prominent of the eyewitness testimonies in this chapter comes from none other than R. A. Torrey (1856–1928). As the successor to the renowned evangelist D. L Moody, Torrey is well placed to provide a balanced assessment of the meetings held by the early Pentecostal movement. Therefore, a significant part of this chapter will focus on Torrey's views. The reason for this is that for the most part, some believe that Torrey may have, through his teaching, inadvertently laid the groundwork for the Pentecostal movement's establishment and its belief of a second baptism. Indeed, it is commonly held that Torrey was the one who developed a stream of teaching (a second experience post-conversion) that some think may well have been a potential precursor to today's version of Pentecostalism. If so, this may well have indirectly provided a basis for the formula on which the Pentecostal movement eventually developed. In the eyes of Torrey, a second experience after salvation was obtainable; however, he did not believe this included speaking in tongues. Therefore, according to this line of reasoning, any second experience was to enable the recipient to receive empowerment for service, albeit minus the miracles. If indeed, as some suppose, Torrey unwittingly created the formula for modern-day Pentecostalism, his stance on the Pentecostal movement was a surprise in that he castigated the Pentecostals' interpretation of his own ideas.¹

TORREY'S TIRADE

The "Tongues Movement" is not of God!² So boomed the words of Torrey, the renowned author of *The Fundamentals* (a series of books defending the Christian faith). The meetings alluded to by Torrey were held at the Azusa Street Mission in Los Angeles. In fact, he inferred that the conduct of these meetings was chaotic, to say the least. Indeed, Torrey was adamant that if God were to orchestrate such things, it would not be with such "disorder, disturbance and confusion," which he observed in some early Pentecostal meetings. When describing these meetings, he alluded to a quote from First Corinthians 14:33, which stated, "God is not a God of confusion."³ Accordingly, Torrey painted a dire picture of what he viewed as a lack of dignity in the meetings. Apparently, as he described, "men and women in large numbers have lain for hours, side by side on the ground or on the platform in the unseemliest and immodest way, in a state of hypnotic consciousness."⁴

Further, Torrey provided a character assessment of the formulator of Pentecostalism, Parham. Although the modesty of the times prevented Torrey from giving an actual description of Parham's alleged indiscretions, he candidly related the following statement:

> The originator in point of time of the modern Tongues Movement was arrested for grossest immorality, a form of immorality for which we have no name in our English language though it is described in the first chapter of Romans.⁵

1. Alexander, *Black Fire*, 136.
2. Torrey, "The Kings Business," 362.
3. Torrey, "The Kings Business," 362.
4. Torrey, "The Kings Business," 362.
5. Torrey, "The Kings Business," 362.

It should be noted at this point, the San Antonio judiciary system later dropped these charges, though it did little for Parham's reputation, as the last chapter will illustrate.

Indeed, so convinced was Torrey that the emerging Pentecostal movement was out-of-step with Bible teaching, he asserted "the tongues movement is a movement upon which God has set the stamp of his disapproval in a most unmistakable way."[6] Further, he stated, "it is a movement that everyone who believes and obeys the word of God should leave severely alone except to expose [it], as there may be occasion."[7]

Concerning the Pentecostal tongues phenomenon, Torrey was not one to limit God. In effect, he maintained that, yes, there might well be the future possibility of God's giving a person in the present day the gift of tongues, only if "God sees fit to do it, he can do it and will do it."[8] Torrey continued that, "God, in His wisdom and love, for a time withdrew this gift from the church and there is no good reason for supposing that he has restored it at the present time."

LOS ANGELES IS ELECTRIFIED

Another prominent eyewitness of early Pentecostalism was a well-respected Methodist minister by the name of W. B. Godbey. While in Los Angeles in 1909, he received an invitation to speak at the Azusa Street Mission. Godbey was a learned man, bilingual (without speaking in tongues) since learning Latin in his mid-twenties. At the ripe of age of seventy-six, Godbey was a well-seasoned preacher. Upon invitation, he duly arrived at the Azusa Street Mission sometime toward the end of 1909. After arriving in Los Angeles, he described the scene that was nothing short of ecstatic. "I found the city on tiptoe, all electrified with the Tongues

---

6. Torrey, "The Kings Business," 362.
7. Torrey, "The Kings Business," 362.
8. Torrey, "The Kings Business," 362.

Movement, the meetings running without intermission day or night," Godbey explained.[9]

Upon entering the city, the Azusa Street people welcomed him warmly. As he stood to speak, the congregation asked whether he had shared their experience of what they referred to as the sign of speaking in tongues. At first, he responded in the affirmative, quoting First Corinthians 14:18, stating, "I can say with Paul; 'I thank my God I speak in tongues more than you all.'"[10] After this, he playfully broke out in perfect Latin; however, those at the Azusa Street meeting house were none the wiser. Godbey, would, for some time continue his charade. In doing so, he allowed them to think he had received the tongues phenomena as well. They were so impressed that they dutifully asked him to become their leader. However, he politely declined the offer and went on his way.[11] A little later upon reflection, he gave a rather candid, if not a caustic, assessment of what he observed at the meetings. They were, as he put it, "Satan's preachers, jugglers, necromancers, enchanters, magicians and all sorts of mendicants, who in all ages have traversed the earth and deceived the people."[12] Adding to the critical tone, Godbey brazenly declared that it was his opinion, "the tongues heresy climaxes all the heresies of all ages in the Holiness Movement."[13]

HYPNOTIC HAPPENINGS?

Another assessment rose from quite a different quarter; only this time it was a little closer to home. Sarah Parham, the wife of Charles, compiled a biography of her husband's life. This work is a credible authority to gain an insight into the mechanics of the early meetings of the Pentecostal movement. For reasons not altogether

9. See Godbey, "Tongue Movement Satanic," 4.
10. See Godbey, "Tongue Movement Satanic," 5.
11. King, *Disfellowshipped*, 43.
12. King, *Disfellowshipped*, 43.
13. See Godbey, "The Tongues Heresy."

clear, Parham narrated the story of a hurried journey to the meetings in Los Angeles late in October 1906. However, some insight into the reasons for Parham's hasty visit is contained in a letter that Seymour addressed to Parham on August 27, 1906:

> Now please let us know about the date that you will be here, so [that] we can advertise your coming and the date... I expect an earthquake to happen in Los Angeles when you come with other workers filled with the Holy Ghost.[14]

From this extract, it seems that at this stage, Parham was a welcome visitor to the Azusa Street meetings. Yet, things soon took a turn for the worse. Indeed, not long after Parham's arrival in Los Angeles, in Seymour's absence, the leaders of the Azusa Street Mission made it known to Parham that he was an unwelcome guest. On the surface, it seems that Seymour's letter was an urgent plea for his mentor Parham to come and help him to differentiate between the real and false activities happening within the early Pentecostal movement. This was in part because of difficulties that had broken loose in the meetings. Soon, however, reminiscent of Seymour's eviction (see chapter 1), Parham became a victim of the same fate after he was kicked out of the venue. What caused such a schism between Seymour and his mentor Parham? It seems that Parham had identified what he viewed as hypnotic happenings at the altar of the Azusa Street Mission. While the meetings at this stage had only been running six months since April, somehow, they had turned into nothing less than chaos unabated by Parham's arrival in October 1906. The founder of the movement then described the scene. Having entered the chapel, he stated that conditions had deteriorated at the Azusa Street Mission beyond imagination. Worse, things had become so out of control that Seymour had "come to me helpless," explained Parham. Apparently, Seymour himself "could not stem the tide that had arisen" within the meetings.[15] All Parham could do upon arrival at the Azusa

---

14. Parham, *The Life of Charles F. Parham*, 154–55.
15. Parham, *The Life of Charles F. Parham*, 163.

Street venue was to sit aghast on the platform watching a scene, he could only describe as, "manifestations of the flesh, spiritualistic controls, and hypnotism at the altar over candidates seeking baptism." Although, he also conceded that "many were receiving the real baptism of the Holy Ghost."[16] Such was the scene that befell the eyes of the man who deserved much of the credit as the architect of the movement. What caused these supposed "hypnotic happenings" to occur? Well, as an interesting aside, Seymour would later (in 1915) make it known that wherever the sign of speaking in tongues becomes the accepted view of the initial evidence of the baptism in the Holy Spirit, then that work could become an "open door for witches, spiritualists" and what he called "free loveism."[17]

It would seem that the door has been already left a little ajar, for according to Parham's biographer James Goff, upon arrival at the venue, Parham became "turned off by the amount of emotional display," so much so, "he prefaced his first remarks at Azusa by declaring unequivocally, God is sick at his stomach!"[18]

THE FIRST PENTECOSTAL CHURCH

Before the birth of modern-day Pentecostalism, there was a movement called, of all things, the Pentecostal Church of the Nazarene. Ironically, this group included the name Pentecostal in its title. Were they of the Pentecostal persuasion? Most definitely not! Although not a Pentecostal church, this particular movement wanted to avoid any confusion of being linked with the newly emerging Pentecostal movement. In fact, the leader, Phineas F. Bresee, promptly changed the name in 1919 from the Pentecostal Church of the Nazarene to simply the Nazarene Church. As a result, they forever erased the term "Pentecostal," from the movement's title.[19]

---

16. Parham, *The Life of Charles F. Parham*, 163.
17. See Robeck, "*The Azusa Street Revival*," 344–45.
18. Goff, *Fields White unto Harvest*, 131.
19. See Sweeden, *Church of the Nazarene*, 578.

The pastor of this church, Bresee, countered claims prevalent in the eyes of many that the Pentecostal movement was the greatest at that time. Rather, he would write, as "represented—in Los Angeles, at least—it is of small moment. It has had, and has now, upon the religious life of the city, about as much influence as a pebble thrown into the sea." Additionally, he described this movement as being locally of "small account," and "being insignificant both in numbers and in influence."[20] However, on the subject of speaking in tongues, Bresee stated that the phenomenon had been a "nothing [nothing]—a jargon, a senseless mumble, without meaning to those who do the mumbling, or to those who hear. Where in a few instances the speaker or some other one has attempted to interpret, it has usually been a poor mess."[21]

Other Christian leaders of the day also added their voices to the rising tide of criticism. Well-known English preacher G. Campbell Morgan, for example, entered the fray, offering a less than positive viewpoint assessment of the early group. The great expositor of the Bible, whom Synan calls "one of the most respected preachers of the twentieth century," brazenly branded the movement as "the last vomit of Satan."[22] Another prominent voice to raise concern, however, came from H. A. Ironside (1876–1951), who previously pastored the Moody Bible Church. He showed even less restraint in his description of the Pentecostal movement, using words such as "disgusting . . . delusions and insanities," and an "unhealthy craving for new and thrilling religious sensations and emotional meetings of a most exciting character." In his estimation, those who "depend so much upon blessings and new baptisms of the Spirit, as they call these experiences . . . readily fall prey to the most absurd delusions."[23]

This chapter has looked at some views, which may be, on balance, considered a little less than positive. That said, as the

---

20. Bangs, *Phineas F. Bresee*, 230.

21. Bangs, *Phineas F. Bresee*, 230.

22. G. Campbell Morgan, as quoted by Synan, *The Holiness-Pentecostal Tradition*, 146.

23. Ironside, *Holiness: The False and the True*, 38–40.

The Pentecostal Paradox

author has shown in previous chapters, the Pentecostal movement is a significant force in the Christian Church. Indeed, its impact is vast, and many genuine people belong to this branch of Christianity. Therefore, Pentecostalism is in every sense sincere in its approach to biblical truth, and mostly, the movement comprises good teaching. There are, however, certain issues that arose in the earlier days of the Pentecostal movement, which the author has tried to address lovingly and sincerely while writing this book. Therefore, in keeping with the tone of this book—as mentioned in chapter 1—the stated aim is to examine the foundations laid at the Azusa Street Mission on April 18, 1906, in Los Angeles. As the book ventures into the final chapter, the focus will be upon; the formulator of modern-day Pentecostalism, Mr. Charles Parham.

9

Parham and the Pentecostal Pandemonium

EARLY PIONEERS OF PENTECOSTALISM believed their movement had no founder but God. In other words, to quote some of their early leaders, the movement's source was from the skies.[1] This fed into the somewhat romantic notion among many of the early Pentecostals that as an organization, "God has raised us up."[2] However, this view seems to be entirely without merit, which even a casual observer soon realizes. Indeed—one person was responsible for the origins of Pentecostalism—Charles Parham. There is another theory about Pentecostalism's roots; as a movement, it only has only spiritual origins. According to this way of thinking, Pentecostalism sprang simultaneously in existence in the context of a broader global revival of Christianity.[3] However, as Goff rightly stated, "this conjecture breaks down because tongues... is traceable directly to Parham."[4] Accordingly, Conkin wrote, "what is incontrovertible is that what happened at Topeka in 1900—1901,

1. Wacker, *Heaven Below*, 142.
2. See McClung, *Truth on Fire*, 82–90.
3. Goff, *Fields White unto Harvest*, 14.
4. Goff, *Fields White unto Harvest*, 14.

The Pentecostal Paradox

had a direct relationship to events on Azusa Street in 1906, and the key individual in these beginnings was Charles F. Parham."[5]

Though few would have heard of him, Charles Parham (1873–1929) was in part responsible for shaping the Pentecostal message. However, as clearly stated in earlier chapters, his protégé William Seymour became the well-known face of the movement and its global distributor. Purdy correctly noted that the Pentecostal movement "has roots in the Bethel Bible College, Topeka, Kansas, under the direction of Charles Fox Parham and the Azusa street revival under the direction of William Seymour."[6]

THE ROOTS OF PENTECOSTALISM

To clearly define a movement, it is necessary first to find its source. This is a crucial step in any historical analysis. If we trace Pentecostalism to its primary source, it starts with the theological founder and father Mr. Charles F. Parham. Therefore, as the founder of the movement, given his character assessment by even their own historians, there remains little doubt that he is shunned as the reputed leader of the Pentecostal movement.

As mentioned in earlier chapters, Parham is the undisputed progenitor of Pentecostalism, as much as Wesley is the father of Methodism, and Luther, the spiritual father of the Lutherans. One stark variance, however, between these leaders relates to the significant points of difference in the theology promoted by each leader. Luther, for example, restored the truth of justification by faith (getting right) and Wesley developed the concept of sanctification (living right). Interestingly, the Pentecostal movement claims it restores the full gospel (e.g., miracles, tongues and other such phenomena from the book of Acts in the Bible).

As noted in chapter 1, the sullied character and somewhat strange beliefs of Parham caused many to view their leader as more of a background figure and not a father figure of the movement.

5. Conkin, *American Originals*, 293.
6. Purdy, *A Distinct Twenty-First Century*, 31.

Parham and the Pentecostal Pandemonium

However, nobody, not even the most ardent Pentecostal, should forget the great debt owed to him for the contribution he made to Pentecostalism. Indeed, we ought to be reminded that it is he who not only licensed his protégé Seymour to preach, he also financed Seymour's trip to Los Angeles in 1906, which lit the spark for Pentecostalism at the inaugural Azusa Street meetings. Without a doubt, wrote Owens, "in its initial phase, Charles Parham was accepted as the leader of the Azusa Street revival."[7]

To put it another way, if there were no Charles Parham, we would not have any such thing as Pentecostalism today. There would be no Azusa Street Mission. Therefore, without a doubt, he is the undisputed leader of the movement.[8]

While both Seymour and Parham together are the pioneers of Pentecostalism, only Parham can correctly bear the label of the founder. Indeed, most historians agree that although he is known as the "formulator" of their movement, most, if not all, Pentecostals would shun calling him the father of it. This is primarily because of questions surrounding his ethics. As a result, his part in the history of Pentecostalism has been greatly "de-emphasized."[9]

PARHAM'S PRECEPTS

Before beginning this section, it is important to note that Pentecostalism's enigmatic leader espoused some rather novel, or at the very least, different teachings than most readers would be comfortable with. Therefore, it stands to reason that the majority of these views would be rejected as a whole by today's Pentecostal movement. In essence, the only aspects of Pentecostalism handed down are the teachings on Spirit baptism.

So then, the following is a catalog of Parham's personally held ideas. At this stage, a short synopsis of these views may suffice, to

---

7. Owens, *The Azusa Street Revival*, 94.
8. Owens, *The Azusa Street Revival*, 94.
9. Synan, *The Holiness-Pentecostal Tradition*, 89.

spare the reader the tedious task of wading through all the details of what he believed and taught.

One of these dubious views he espoused, which, according to his wife Sarah, included belonging to a Freemasonry Lodge, alarmingly, there is evidence of this in a biographical sketch published one year after his death in 1930. The title of the book is *The Life of Charles F. Parham, Founder of the Apostolic Faith Movement.* In this text, a rather intriguing entry stated, "Mr. Parham belonged to a Lodge [Freemasonry] and carried an insurance on his life."[10] So, did he give this up? Well, he said that he would give it up since later in his life story, it stated, "he felt now that he should give this up also as it would seem inconsistent with his faith."[11] However, much later in his life's story, there is a seemingly contradictory statement that he "was going to present a gavel to the Masonic Lodge in Baxter Springs" with his respects.[12] Among other controversial views, Parham was, to some extent, sympathetic to the controversial Ku Klux Klan, whom he called "those splendid men" having preached to them on occasions.[13] In light of this, MacArthur explained that Parham was, at times, "attracted to the teachings that were marginal, novel, extreme or totally unorthodox."[14]

Another questionable belief was the rejection of any medicine in favor of faith healing. According to Goff, "Parham's opposition to medical science went deeper than skepticism about the success of certain treatments. Parham believed that taking medicine was wrong."[15] Alarmingly, Parham became so adamant that this was the case; he interpreted his experience as universally applicable, claiming to have Bible evidence for this assumption.[16]

Another misconstrued notion was the belief in the eventual annihilation of the wicked, or what is more commonly known as

10. Parham, *The Life of Charles F. Parham*, 32.
11. Parham, *The Life of Charles F. Parham*, 32.
12. Parham, *The Life of Charles F. Parham*, 373.
13. Hollenweger and MacRobert, *The Black Roots*, 62.
14. MacArthur, *Strange Fire*, 25.
15. Goff, *Fields White unto Harvest*, 43.
16. Goff, *Fields White unto Harvest*, 43.

conditional immortality. Indeed, by holding this view, he contended that although the non-Christians will face some sort of judgment, this oddly enough would end their existence by total annihilation in the future life.[17] In other words, the founder of the Pentecostal movement denied the long-held clear biblical teaching of eternal damnation.

Perhaps most disturbing of all is the view, which Parham nurtured about the phenomenon of speaking in tongues concerning end-time events. This notion of the so-called sealing for the rapture was indeed an unusual belief. According to this view, only those who hold to the traditional Pentecostal practice of speaking in tongues would be safe from the plagues that he assumed would come upon the earth in the last days. Therefore, the so-called Pentecostal Spirit Baptism was a special seal of God's approval, ensuring one's place in the new age.[18] At the same time, only an "elite band" of Christians (i.e., those who speak in tongues) would ultimately be snatched away at the return of Christ.[19] Therefore, Parham so taught that those with the Pentecostal sign of speaking in tongues would be the only ones spared the awful trials of what he believed would be the end-times seven-year tribulation period. Hence, they would then take up important positions in the millennial (i.e., 1,000 years) government.[20]

Parham was set apart not only by his unorthodox beliefs but also by his uniqueness, which as the following section will show, have little or no precedence in church history. For example, one of his misconstrued views stated that God created two separate species of humanity. This is, of course, directly opposed to the biblical account. However, from this point, his belief system becomes even more skewed. He stated that not all humanity sprang from Adam and Eve according to the biblical account. According to this view, there were two different species of humankind created one on the

---

17. Goff, *Fields White unto Harvest*, 35.
18. Goff, *Fields White unto Harvest*, 78.
19. Parham, *A Voice Crying*, 93.
20. Goff, *Fields White unto Harvest*, 78.

sixth day and another on the eighth day of creation.[21] In Parham's eyes, maintaining the idea of two separate species of humans would reconcile the creation accounts in the first two chapters of the book of Genesis.[22]

Along with this belief, he also maintained that those created on the sixth day had what he termed "everlasting human life," while the rest of humanity created on the eighth day (i.e., Adam, Eve and their descendants) were merely only capable of receiving everlasting life.[23] On the sixth day, people apparently were created in God's image; on the eighth day, people whom he called the inferior race were formed of the dust.[24] For this reason, wrote Espinosa, "Parham believed it was important to segregate the races and avoid interracial marriage because miscegenation had caused the flood."[25]

As reprehensible as these views are today, no doubt most Pentecostals would repudiate this type of dogma. Whatever the case, these views were, nonetheless, part of Parham's belief system. Therefore, whether they "like it or not," as MacArthur reasoned, "contemporary Pentecostals (and by extension, all Charismatics) are stuck with Charles Parham."[26] Accordingly, along with the belief of the original creation comprising two separate species of humanity, apparently, the so-called "sixth-day" people began well; however, after Adam and Eve's expulsion from the Garden of Eden, they then dwelt among whom Parham called the "inferior first creation."[27]

What of the Garden of Eden? Well, according to the master of speculation, Parham, apparently the lost city of Atlantis is the former Eden.[28] After Adam and Eve's expulsion from Eden, their son

21. Jacobson, *Thinking in the Spirit*, 29.
22. Jacobson, *Thinking in the* Spirit, 29.
23. Parham, The Everlasting Gospel, 20.
24. Goff, *Fields White unto Harvest*, 103.
25. See Espinosa, "Ordinary Prophet," 35.
26. MacArthur, *Strange Fire*, 27.
27. Goff, *Fields White unto Harvest*, 103.
28. Goff, *Fields White unto Harvest*, 103.

PARHAM AND THE PENTECOSTAL PANDEMONIUM

Cain supposedly disrupted the tranquility that existed. After his brother Abel's death, Parham speculated that Cain fled to the land of Nod to live among the so-called sixth-day people.[29] Apparently, after this, when the sixth-day people saw the eighth-day people (the Adamic race),[30] they intermarried and—in his mind—this apparently led to the flood in Noah's day as a punishment for the mingling of the races who in Parham's words "were no longer worthy of any existence."[31] This, in the mind of the ever-speculative Parham, finally put to rest the age-old question of where Cain found a wife, as he supposedly intermarried with the sixth-day people.[32]

RETRIEVING THE LOST ARK

Adding to the plethora of radical theories endorsed by Parham, and perhaps the most intriguing of all is the supposed unraveling of the age-old mystery of the lost Ark of the Covenant. As such, he taught that the Ark alone held the key to the return of the Jewish race to Israel, which in turn, would hasten a massive migration. Hence, in his mind, the restored Ten Commandments and the recovered Ark would become a symbol of the time of the Jewish restoration. This would trigger a massive Aliyah, or return to Israel. If that was not enough, he then boldly announced that he also knew the whereabouts of Noah's Ark, supposedly from information gleaned from a tip he received from an "old Jewish document."[33] Indeed, the crowds listened with rapt attention, as he explained that he would try to retrieve Noah's Ark, and in 1908, he began a fundraising campaign in trying to unravel this age-old mystery. To this end, he began trumpeting the plan to the newspapers to garner support for what would become his most ill-fated

---

29. Parham, *A Voice Crying*, 88.
30. Parham, *A Voice Crying*, 88–89.
31. Parham, The Everlasting Gospel, 22.
32. Synan and Fox, *William J. Seymour*, 366.
33. Goff, *Fields White unto Harvest*, 102.

venture to date. He would, he believed, single-handedly attempt an archaeological expedition to Israel in trying to win Pentecostal affection. The venture, if successful, he believed would re-establish his position as the "best-known Pentecostal in America."[34] According to Parham's biographer Goff, "After parading the plan before the press and raising sufficient funds, Parham journeyed to New York in December 1908 to board a steamer for Jerusalem."[35] Having raised sufficient funds for the venture, all that was necessary was to put the plan into action. However, the only problem was, apparently, he fell afoul of thieves in New York and never managed to purchase that ticket for the Middle East. To no one's surprise, he returned to Kansas in January 1909, minus the funds, to tell his sad tale.[36]

In all the above cases, clearly, Parham as a Pentecostal pioneer has a disjointed record of accomplishment. To put it another way, eventually, the instigator of Pentecostalism would become less of an asset and more of an embarrassment to his followers. Only time will tell if the movement he developed will relinquish or relish its connection with Parham.

Eventually, of course, his reputation suffered. This was, in part due to a situation that arose (only one year after the Azusa Street movement began) in 1907. At this time, he faced arrest in San Antonio, Texas (see chapter 8). The fallout was even worse, in that the charge, although eventually dropped, caused a suspicion to hang over both the man and the movement leaving Parham's reputation tarnished.[37] After this, many within Pentecostalism distanced themselves from their founder while others became disillusioned, pursuing various other interests. Therefore, it was not long before Parham faced not only "personal tragedy," but along with this also came "public rejection."[38]

---

34. Goff, *Fields White unto Harvest*, 146.
35. Goff, *Fields White unto Harvest*, 146.
36. Goff, *Fields White unto Harvest*, 146.
37. See Espinosa, "Ordinary Prophet," 50.
38. Blumhofer, *Restoring the Faith*, 53.

PARHAM AND THE PENTECOSTAL PANDEMONIUM

So, what happened to Parham's theology? Well, as mentioned previously, Seymour inherited only the tongues theology from Parham and proceeded to spread it through the Azusa Street Mission. As a result, Parham, in part at least, shaped the Pentecostal message and as mentioned earlier, Seymour globally distributed it.[39]

END OF THE PARHAM LEGACY

Although Parham's legacy among Pentecostals is undeniable, sadly, the origins of the Pentecostal movement would continue without referring to their own founder. Indeed, the Pentecostal leader would live out the rest of his days as an enigmatic figure within the very movement he helped establish. The General Council of the AG explained Barfoot, erased his name "for years in the repetition of the mythology of their origins."[40] According to Goff, until Parham's death in 1929, he was almost unknown among the developing second generation of the Pentecostal denominations, which he founded. However, soon this changed, and eventually, he received the due recognition, but that did not occur until after the Second World War when the Pentecostal movement thrived. At this time, Parham would now be regarded, as biographer Goff put it, "an important religious pioneer of the twentieth century."[41]

In already declining health in 1927, Parham took a long trip to the Middle East, returning home the following year in April 1928. This would be his final journey abroad.

On January 29, 1929, aged 56, Parham passed away with his life's work leaving an ongoing legacy. In keeping with his convictions, he refused any medical intervention in his last hours. After his passing, the Pentecostal movement was left divided, without becoming the unifying revival of religion Parham expected. According to Parham's biographer:

---

39. Purdy, *A Distinct Twenty-First Century*, 30.
40. Barfoot, *Aimee Semple McPherson*, 134.
41. Goff, *Fields White unto Harvest*, 159.

The man who had established their theological identity almost three decades earlier had been lost amid scandal and doctrinal debate. The mass end time revival that had promised Christian unity in 1901 had failed to materialize.[42]

What happened to William Seymour and the Azusa Street Mission house? Well, Seymour passed away September 28, 1922, having suffered a heart attack at fifty-two years of age. After this, his wife Jenny took over as pastor of the congregation, which she oversaw until they demolished the building in 1931.

Despite these humble endings, Pentecostalism has become a pervasive worldwide movement. This book has presented a well-referenced comprehensive narrative history. After reading this book, it is hoped that the reader will develop a better understanding of the colorful and complex history of the fastest growing movement in the contemporary world.

---

42. Goff, *Fields White unto Harvest*, 159.

Conclusion

WE LIVE IN AN era where people rarely have time to read large and voluminous books. Therefore, I realized that there was a need for a smaller and more compact version of Pentecostalism. One written not by insiders, but by an outside observer, offering the reader a real glimpse into the inner workings of the Pentecostal movement. As such, I have tried to put together an easy-to-read, well-referenced historical account explaining not only the origins of the Pentecostal movement but also some issues surrounding the movement's rise which many contemporary works do not seem to cover.

Given that many books during the last century have addressed the subject of Pentecostalism since its beginnings, the reader may ask what need is there for another? However, any informed reader will soon discover that out of the vast array of Pentecostal literature on offer today; many of these portray a rather romanticized history of the movement. Therefore, books like this one are needed to allow the reader to gain a balanced view of the Pentecostal movement's development and beliefs throughout the last century. This is especially so when looking at its origins, enabling the reader to gain a balanced and unbiased view of the Pentecostal movement's formation and establishment.

I write this primarily for those who may have lingering questions about the movement. They will find *The Pentecostal Paradox* is an invaluable tool in guiding them through the maze of issues confronting the Pentecostal movement at the moment. It is hoped these writings will also appeal to the broader Evangelical community and those on the periphery of Christendom as well. For many of these readers, most of the material written on Pentecostalism is either inaccessible, unavailable, or perhaps written in a way that may not engage them. Accordingly, I have been conscious while writing this history of the movement that it needs to be in plain terms making it accessible to the general reader. Particularly those who may not understand Pentecostalism, and as a result, stand aloof from the movement because of preconceived misconceptions.

Some, having read this book may conjecture that its findings are one-sided. However, this book has tried to side with the Bible and church history, which is always the best standard for doctrinal analysis and this is especially so when considering any new teaching that is introduced into the church.

So, now you have finished reading this book, you may still have lingering questions relating to the Pentecostal movement and its establishment. However, by comparing biblical truths with historical evidence, (as this book has tried to do), the answer to these questions can quickly be resolved.

It is my prayer, indeed, my utmost desire that many other books of this type will follow, allowing readers to gain a balanced perception of this new religious phenomenon, which has taken the world by storm during the last century or so.

Bibliography

Adogame, Afe. "Pentecostal and Charismatic Movements in a Global Perspective." In *The New Blackwell Companion to the Sociology of Religion*, edited by Bryan S. Turner, 498–520. West Sussex, United Kingdom: Wiley Blackwell, 2010.

Alexander, Estrelda. *The Women of Azusa Street*. Cleveland, Ohio: Pilgrim,, 2005.

Anderson, Alan Heaton. *To the Ends of the Earth: Pentecostalism of and the Transformation of World Christianity*. Oxford, United Kingdom: Oxford University Press, 2013.

———. *An Introduction to Pentecostalism: Global Charismatic Christianity*. Cambridge, United Kingdom: Cambridge University Press, 2004.

———. "Varieties, Taxonomies, and Definitions." In *Studying Global Pentecostalism: Theories and Methods*, edited by Anderson, Allen et al., 13–28. Berkeley: University of California Press, 2010.

Archer, Kenneth J. *The Gospel Revisited: Towards a Pentecostal Theology of Worship and Witness*. Eugene, Oregon: Pickwick, 2011.

Armstrong, John H. "In Search of Spiritual Power." In *Power Religion: The Selling Out of the Evangelical Church*, edited by Michael Scott Horton, 60–88. Chicago: Moody, 1992.

Arnott, John. *The Father's Blessing*. Lake Mary, Florida: Creation House, 1996.

Assemblies of God. "The 57th Session of the General Council with Revised Constitution and Bylaws." https://ag.org/About/About-the-AG/Constitution-and-Bylaws. Anaheim, California.

———. "Manifestations of the Spirit." https://ag.org/Beliefs/Topics-Index/Manifestations-of-the-Spirit.

———. Paper. "Baptism in the Holy Spirit." https://ag.org/Beliefs/Position-Papers/Baptism-in-the-Holy-Spirit.

———. "Pentecostal Outpouring." *Pentecostal Evangel* 4261–86 (2006) 27.

Augustine, Saint. *Homilies on the Gospel According to St. John: And His First Epistle*. Vol. 2. Oxford, United Kingdom: Baxter, 1849.

Bangs, Carl. *Phineas F. Bresee: His Life in Methodism, the Holiness Movement and the Church of the Nazarene*. Kansas City: Beacon, 1995.

Bibliography

Banks, Adelle M. "Poll Says Many Pentecostals Don't Speak in Tongues." *Christianity Today*, October 6, 2006. https://www.christianitytoday.com/ct/2006/octoberweb-only/140-53.0.html.

Barbare, Donald R. *The 80% Solution: Christians Doing the Right Thing*. Bloomington, Indiana: Xlibris, 2012.

Barfoot, Chas H. *Aimee Semple McPherson and the Making of Modern Pentecostalism, 1890-1926*. London: Routledge, 2014.

Barna Group. "Is American Christianity Turning Charismatic?" January 2008. https://www.barna.com/research/is-american-christianity-turning-charismatic/.

Barnes, Roscoe III. *F. F. Bosworth: The Man Behind Christ the Healer*. Newcastle upon Tyne, United Kingdom: Cambridge Scholars, 2009.

Barret, David B., and Johnson Todd. M. "Global Statistics." In *The New International Dictionary of Pentecostal and Charismatic Movements*, edited by Stanley Burgess, and Eduard Van Der Mass, 284-302. Grand Rapids, Michigan: Zondervan, 2002.

———. "World Christian Trends, AD 30–AD 2200: Interpreting the Annual Christian Mega Census." Pasadena, California: William Carey Library, 2001.

Bartleman, Frank. *Azusa Street, an Eyewitness Account to the Birth of the Pentecostal Revival*. New Kensington, Pennsylvania: Whitaker House, 1982.

Benton, Joseph A. *Pacific School of Religion, Joseph Augustine Benton: In Memorial*. Berkeley, California: Pacific, 1892.

Beveridge, Henry, ed. *John Calvin, Commentary upon the Acts of the Apostles*, vol. 1 Edinburgh, London: Edinburgh, 1844.

Beverley, James A. "Dental Miracle Reports Draw Criticism." *Christianity Today*, May 24, 1999. https://www.christianitytoday.com/ct/1999/may24/9t617a.html.

———. "Vineyard Severs Ties with Toronto Blessing Church." *Christianity Today*, January 8, 1996. https://www.christianitytoday.com/ct/1996/january8/6t1066.html.

Blumhofer, Edith Waldvogel. *Restoring the Faith: The Assemblies of God, Pentecostalism, and American Culture*. Illinois: University of Illinois Press, 1993.

———. "Restoration as Revival." In *Modern Christian Revivals*, edited by Edith Waldvogel Blumhofer and Randall Herbert Balmer, 145-60. Urbana, Illinois: University of Illinois Press, 1993.

Borlase, Craig. *William Seymour: A Biography*. Lake Mary, Florida: Charisma, 2006.

Brands, H.W. *The Age of Gold: The California Gold Rush and the New American Dream*. New York: Doubleday, 2002.

Bruner, Dale F. *A Theology of the Holy Spirit, the Pentecostal Experience and the New Witness*. Eugene, Oregon: Wipf and Stock, 1970.

BIBLIOGRAPHY

Campbell, Marne L. *Making Black Los Angeles: Class, Gender, and Community, 1850–1917.* Chapel Hill, North Carolina: University of North Carolina Press, 2016.

Campolo, Tony. *How to Be Pentecostal without Speaking in Tongues.* Dallas, Texas: Word, 1991.

Carson, D. A. *Showing the Spirit: A Theological Exposition of 1 Corinthians 12–14.* Grand Rapids, Michigan: Baker, 2019.

Chan, Simon. *Pentecostal Theology and the Christian Spiritual Tradition.* Eugene, Oregon: Wipf and Stock, 2000.

Chesnut, R Andrew. *Born Again in Brazil: The Pentecostal Boom and the Pathogens of Poverty.* New Brunswick, New Jersey: Rutgers University Press, 1977.

Chevreau, Guy. *Catch the Fire: The Toronto Blessing: An Experience of Renewal and Revival.* London: Marshall, 1994.

Choi, Meesaeng Lee. "Healing." In *The Encyclopedia of Christianity in the United States*, edited by Thomas George Kurian and Mark A. Lamport, 5, 1062–69. Maryland, London: Rowman & Littlefield, 2016.

Christerson, Brad and Richard Flory. *The Rise of Network Christianity: How Independent Leaders Are Changing the Religious Landscape.* New York: Oxford University Press, 2017.

Chrysostom, Saint John. *Homilies of Saint John Chrysostom, Archbishop of Constantinople, First Epistle of St Paul the Apostle to the Corinthians.* Oxford, London: Baxter, 1839.

Conkin, Paul K. *American Originals: Homemade Varieties of Christianity.* Chapel Hill, North Carolina: University of North Carolina Press, 1997.

Copeland, Kenneth. *The Force of Faith.* Ft. Worth, Texas: Copeland, 1983.

Cottrell, Jack. *The Holy Spirit: A Biblical Study.* Joplin, Missouri: College, 2006.

Cox, Harvey. *Fire from Heaven, the Rise of Pentecostal Spirituality and the Reshaping of Religion in the 21st Century.* Reading, Massachusetts: Addison-Wesley, 1995.

Creech, Joe. "Visions of Glory: The Place of the Azusa Street Revival in Pentecostal History." *Church History* 65, 3 (1996) 405–424.

Creemers, Jelle. *Theological Dialogue with Classical Pentecostals.* London: T. & T. Clark, 2015.

Dager, Albert James. "Holy Laughter: Rodney Howard-Browne and the Toronto Blessing." *Media Spotlight*, 1995. http://www.mediaspotlight.org/pdfs/HOLY%20LAUGHTER.pdf.

Dart, John. "Reverend Got Tongue Lashing for Beliefs." *Los Angeles Daily Times*, July 3, 1997. http://articles.latimes.com/1997/jul/03/local/me-9454.

Davenport, Keith. *Azusa Revisited.* New York: Lulu, 2008.

Davis, Mike. "L. A's Pentecostal Earthquake," *Grand Street Symbols* 68, 17 (1999).

Dayton, Donald W. "The Limits of Evangelicalism: The Pentecostal Tradition." In *The Variety of American Evangelicalism*, edited by Donald W. Dayton,

and Robert K. Johnston, 36–56. Knoxville: University of Tennessee Press, 1991.
Dempster, M.W. "Pacifism in Pentecostalism." In *The Fragmentation of the Church and its Unity in Peacemaking*, edited by Jeffrey Gros, and John D. Rempel, 137–65. Grand Rapids, Michigan: Eerdmans, 2001.
Dueck, Lorna. "The Enduring Revival." *Christianity Today*, March 7, 2014. https://www.christianitytoday.com/ct/2014/march-web-only/enduring-revival.html.
Economist. "Pentecostals: Christianity Reborn." 38, December 19, 2006.
Eifler, Mark A. *The California Gold Rush: The Stampede That Changed the World*. New York: Routledge, 2017.
Epting, Charles. *Victorian Los Angeles*. Charleston, South Carolina: History, 2015.
Espinosa, Gaston. "Ordinary Prophet: William. J. Seymour and the Azusa Street Revival." In *The Azusa Street Revival and its Legacy*, edited by Harold Hunter, and Cecil M. Robeck Jr., 29–60. Cleveland, Ohio: Pathway, 2006.
Estrelda, Alexander Y. *Black Fire: One Hundred Years of African American Pentecostalism*. Downers Grove, Illinois: Intervarsity, 2011.
Falsani, Cathleen. "The Worst Ideas of the Decade. The Prosperity Gospel." *Washington Post*, 2009. http://www.washingtonpost.com/wp-srv/special/opinions/outlook/worst-ideas/prosperity-gospel.html.
Fenwick, Peter. "Prophecy Today." *Blessing the Church*? December 1, 2017. https://prophecytoday.uk/study/teaching-articles/item/903-blessing-the-church-vi.html
Flynn, Leslie B. *19 Gifts of the Spirit*. Colorado Springs, Colorado: David C. Cook, 1994.
Fradkin, Phillip L. *The Great Earthquake and Firestorms of 1906*. Berkeley: University of California Press, 2005.
French, Talmadge L. *Early Interracial Oneness Pentecostalism: G. T. Haywood and the Pentecostal Assemblies of the World*. Eugene, Oregon: Pickwick, 2013.
Friedman, Robert, ed. "The Life Millennium: The 100 Most Important Events and People of the Past 1000 Years." New York: Life, 1998.
Friesen, Aaron. *Norming the Abnormal: The Development and Function of the Doctrine of Initial Evidence in Classical Pentecostalism*. Eugene, Oregon: Pickwick, 2013.
Fudge, T. A. *Christianity without the Cross: A History of Salvation in Oneness Pentecostalism*. Parkland, Florida: Universal, 2013.
Gardiner, George E. *The Corinthian Catastrophe*. Grand Rapids, Michigan: Kregel, 1974.
Garrett, James Leo, Jr. *Systematic Theology: Biblical, Historical, and Evangelical*. Vol 2. Eugene, Oregon: Wipf and Stock, 1990.
Gladden, Washington. "Back to Pentecost." In *The Biblical World*, edited by Harper, William Rainey et al., 50, 203–210, 1919.

BIBLIOGRAPHY

Godbey, William Baxter. "Tongue Movement Satanic." In *Six Tracts*, edited by Donald Dayton, 1–6. New York: Garland, 1985.

———. "The Tongues Heresy." In *Pillar of Fire: 1987–1988*. Madison, Wisconsin: University of Wisconsin Press, 2010.

Goff, James R. Jr. *Fields White unto Harvest: Charles F. Parham and the Missionary Origins of Pentecostalism*. Fayetteville, Arkansas: University of Arkansas Press, 1988.

Goodman, Walter. "Television Review: About Churches, Souls, and Show Biz Methods." *New York Times*, 16 March 1995.

Goodstein, Laurie. "Believers Invest of the Gospel of Getting Rich." *New York Times*, August 15, 2009. https://www.nytimes.com/2009/08/16/us/16gospel.html.

Govan, Chloe. *The Incredible Rise of Mumford & Sons*. London: Omnibus, 2013.

Grady, J. Lee. *The Holy Spirit is Not for Sale: Rekindling the Power of God in an Age of Compromise*. Grand Rapids, Michigan: Chosen, 2010.

———. "What Happened to the Brownsville's Fire?" *CBN*. http://www1.cbn.com/spirituallife/what-happened-to-brownsville%27s-fire.

———. "Life after Lakeland: Sorting out the Confusion." August 13, 2008. http://enjoyingthejourney.blogspot.com/2008/08/charismas-editor-lee-grady-talks-about.html.

Graham, Billy. *The Collected Works of Billy Graham*. New York: Inspirational, 1993.

Grenz. Stanley J. *Theology for the Community of God*. Grand Rapids, Michigan: Eerdmans, 2000.

Gryboski, Michael. "Assemblies of God Leader Denies That Speaking in Tongues is in Decline in Pentecostal Churches." *Christian Post*, September 3, 2013. https://www.christianpost.com/news/assemblies-of-god-leader-denies-that-speaking-in-tongues-is-in-decline-in-pentecostal-churches-103613/.

Hagin, Kenneth E. *How to Write Your Own Ticket with God*. Faith Library, 1979.

Hanegraaff, Hank. *Counterfeit Revival: Looking for God in all the Wrong Places*. Nashville, Tennessee: Thomas Nelson, 1999.

Harrell, Gaustad et al. "In the Sixties and Seventies." In *Unto a Good Land: A History of the American People, Volume 2: From 1865*. Grand Rapids, Michigan: Eerdmans, 2005.

Hayford, Jack W., and David S. Moore. *The Charismatic Century: The Enduring Impact of the Azusa Street Revival*. New York: Warner, 2009.

Hinn, Costi W., and Wood, Anthony G. *Defining Deception: Freeing the Church from the Mystical-Miracle Movement*. El Cajon, California: Southern California Seminary Press, 2018.

Hoekema, Anthony A. *What about Tongue Speaking?* Grand Rapids, Michigan: Eerdmans, 1966.

Hocken, Peter. "Charismatic Movement." In *The New International Dictionary of Pentecostal and Charismatic Movements*, edited by Stanley Burgess, and

Bibliography

Eduard Van der Maas, 477–519. Grand Rapids, Michigan: Zondervan, 2002.

Holland, Clifton L. *The Religious Dimension in Hispanic Los Angeles: A Protestant Case Study.* South Pasadena, California: William Carey Library, 1974.

Hollenweger, Walter J., and Iain MacRobert. *The Black Roots and White Racism of Early Pentecostalism in the USA.* London: Macmillan, 1988.

Holliday, J. S. *The World Rushed in: The California Gold Rush Experience.* Norman, Oklahoma: University of Oklahoma Press, 1999.

Horton, Greg, and Shimron Yonat. "Southern Baptists to Open their Ranks to Missionaries Who Speak in Tongues." *Washington Post*, May 14, 2015. https://www.washingtonpost.com/national/religion/southern-baptists-to-open-their-ranks-to-missionaries-who-speak-in-tongues/2015/05/14/1fddd28a-fa7e-11e4-a47c-e56f4db884ed_story.html?utm_term=.ef660e35e8ca.

Hummel, Charles E. *Fire in the Fireplace: Charismatic Renewal in the Nineties.* Downers Grove, Illinois: Intervarsity, 1993.

Hunt, Stephan. "The Toronto Blessing: A Lesson Globalized Religion." In *Canadian Pentecostalism: Transition and Transformation*, edited by Michael Wilkinson, 237–248. Montreal, Canada: McGill-Queens University Press, 2009.

———. "Forty Years of Millenarian Thought in the Charismatic Movement." In *Expecting the End, Millennialism in Social and Historical Context*, edited by Kenneth G. C. Newport, and Crawford Gribben, 193–212. Waco, Texas: Baylor University Press, 2006.

Hunter, Harold D. *Spirit Baptism: A Pentecostal Alternative.* Eugene, Oregon: Wipf and Stock, 2009.

Hyatt, Eddie, ed. *Fire on the Earth: Eyewitness Reports from the Azusa Street Revival.* Lake Mary, Florida: Creation House, 2006.

Irenaeus, Bishop of Lyon. *The Writings of Irenaeus.* Vol. 9. Edinburgh: T & T Clarke, 1869.

Ironside, Harry A. *Holiness: The False and the True.* Neptune, New Jersey: Loizeaux, 1912.

Jacobson, Douglass. *Global Gospel, an Introduction to Christianity on Five Continents.* Grand Rapids, Michigan: Baker, 2015.

———. *Thinking in the Spirit: Theologies of the Early Pentecostal Movement.* Bloomington, Indiana: Indiana University Press, 2000.

Johns, Kenneth D. *The Pentecostal Paradigm: A Seductive Paradise.* Bloomington, Indiana: Xlibris, 2007.

Johnson, Todd M., et al. "Christianity 2017: Five Hundred Years of Protestant Christianity." *International Bulletin of Mission Research* 41.1 (2017) 41–52.

———. "The Demographics of Revival." In *Spirit-Empowered Christianity in the 21st Century: Insights, Analysis, and Future Trends.*, edited by Synan, Vinson, 55–69. Lake Mary, Florida: Charisma House, 2011.

Jurgensmeier, Kurt. *Book 5 Apologetics P B How Does God Really Want Us to Prove Christianity?* Cedar Rapids Iowa: Training Timothys, 2012.

BIBLIOGRAPHY

———. *Book 10 God's Miracles: How Does God Supernaturally Reveal Himself?* Cedar Rapids, Iowa: Training Timothys. 2012.
King, David W. *The Bible in History: How the Texts Have Shaped the Times.* New York: Oxford University Press, 2004.
King, Gerald W. *Disfellowshipped: Pentecostal Responses to Fundamentalism in the United States, 1906-1943.* Eugene, Oregon: Pickwick, 2011.
Kostlevy, William. *Holy Jumpers: Evangelicals and Radicals in Progressive Era America.* New York: Oxford University Press, 2010.
———. *The A to Z of the Holiness Movement.* Plymouth, United Kingdom: Scarecrow, 2009.
Kuyper, Abraham. *The Work of the Holy Spirit.* New York: Cosimo, 2007.
Larkin, Clarence. *Dispensational Truth, or God's Plan and Purpose in the Ages.* New York: Cosimo, 2010.
Latourette, Kenneth S. *A History of Christianity.* Peabody, Massachusetts: Hendrickson, 1975,
Lawrence, B. F. "Back to Pentecost." In *Three Early Pentecostal Tracts*, edited by D. W. Dayton, 12-15. New York: Garland, 1985.
Le Beau, Bryant. *A History of Religion in America: From the End of the Civil War to the Twenty-First Century.* New York: Routledge, 2017.
Liardon, Roberts. *The Azusa Street Revival: When the Fire Fell: An In-Depth Look at the People, Teachings and Lessons.* Shippensburg, Pennsylvania: Destiny, 2006.
Logan, William Bryant, and Susan Ochshorn, "Los Angeles and Southern California." In *The Smithsonian Guide to Historic America: Pacific States*, edited by Roger G. Kennedy, 21-102. New York: Stewart, Tabori & Chang, 1989.
Los Angeles Herald. "How Holy Roller Gets Religion." September 10, 33 (1906) 345.
———. "Population is Past 230, 000." April 15, 33 (1906) 197.
Los Angeles Times. "Weird Babel of Tongues," April 18, 1906.
Lovelace, Libby. "Lifeway Releases Prayer Language Study." *BP News*, June 1, 2007. http://www.bpnews.net/25765/lifeway-releases-prayer-language-study.
Lausanne Theology Working Group. "A Statement on the Prosperity Gospel." January 6, 2010. https://www.lausanne.org/content/a-statement-on-the-prosperity-gospel.
Lugo, Luis and John Green. Pew Research Center, press conference, Los Angeles, California. October 2006. http://www.pewforum.org/2006/10/05/spirit-and-power-news-conference/
Lutzer, Erwin W. *Who Are You to Judge? Learning to Distinguish Between Truths, Half-Truths and Lies.* Chicago, Illinois: Moody, 2002
MacArthur, John, ed. "All That Glitters, A Call for Biblical Discernment." In *Fools Gold? Discerning Truth from Error.* Wheaton, Illinois: Crossway, 2005.

Bibliography

―――. "Tongue Tied, Part 2." Grace to You. October 10, 2013. https://www.gty.org/library/blog/B131010.

―――. *Charismatic Chaos*. Grand Rapids, Michigan: Zondervan, 1992.

―――. *Strange Fire: The Danger of Offending the Holy Spirit with Counterfeit Worship*. Nashville, Tennessee: Nelson, 2013.

Marsden, George M. *Reforming Fundamentalism*. Grand Rapids, Michigan: Eerdmans, 1987.

Maseko, Achim N. *Church Schism & Corruption*. Durban, South Africa: Lulu, 2008.

Maxwell, Joe. "Is Laughing for the Lord Holy?" *Christianity Today*, October 24, 1994. https://www.christianitytoday.com/ct/1994/october24/4tco78.html.

McClung, Grant, ed. "Historical Perspectives." In *Azusa Street and Beyond: Pentecostal Missions and Church Growth in the Twentieth Century*. Alachua, Florida: Bridge Logos, 2012.

―――. "Truth on Fire: Pentecostals and an Urgent Missiology." In *Azusa Street and Beyond*. Alachua, Florida: Bridge Logos, 2005.

McGee, Gary B. "The Calcutta Revival of 1907 and the Reformulation of Charles F. Parham's 'Bible Evidence' Doctrine." *AJPS* 6, 1 (2003) 123-43.

Melton, Gordon J, ed. "Seymour, William J." In the *Encyclopedia of Protestantism*, 492-93. New York: Facts on File, 2005.

―――. "William Seymour." In *Religions of the World: A Comprehensive Encyclopedia of Beliefs and Practices*, edited by Gordon J. Melton, and Martin Baumann, 1, 2593-94. Santa Barbara, California: ABC-CLIO, 2010.

―――. "Dentistry Paranormal." In *The Encyclopedia of Religious Phenomena*, 87-88. Canton, Michigan: Visible Ink, 2008.

Menzies, William W. *Anointed to Serve: The Story of the Assemblies of God*. Springfield, Missouri: Gospel, 1971.

Mills, Watson E, ed. *Speaking in Tongues: A Guide to Research on Glossolalia*. Grand Rapids, Michigan: Eerdmans, 1986.

Mittelstadt, Martin William. "Reimaging Luke-Acts Amos Yong and the Biblical Foundation of Pentecostal Theology." In *The Theology of Amos Yong and the New Face of Pentecostal Scholarship: Passion for the Spirit*, edited by Wolfgang Vondey and Martin W. Mittelstadt, 25-43. Leiden, Netherlands: Brill, 2013.

Mohler, Albert. "News Note: The Death of Oral Roberts." December 16, 2009. https://albertmohler.com/2009/12/16/newsnote-the-death-of-oral-roberts/

Montier, Gerald, and Carolyn Montier. *Remembering the Past: Apostolic Faith Mission Celebrating the Present Apostolic Faith Church of God*. Bloomington, Indiana: Xlibris, 2011.

Moody, David. *Spirit of the Living God: What the Bible Says About the Spirit*. Nashville, Tennessee: Bradman, 1976.

BIBLIOGRAPHY

Moore, David. "Discerning the Times: The Victorious Eschatology Shepherding Movement." In *Pentecostal Eschatology: World without End*, edited by Peter Althouse, and Robby Waddell, 273–92. Eugene, Oregon: Pickwick, 2010.
Morris, McCowan, et al. *They Told Me Their Stories: The Youth and Children of Azusa Street Tell Their Stories*. Mustang, Oklahoma: Dare2Dream, 2006.
Newman, Larry Vern. *The Ultimate Evidence: Rethinking the Evidence Issues for Spirit-Baptism*. Eugene, Oregon: Wipf and Stock, 2009.
New York Times. "The San Francisco Earthquake." March 12, 2011, 13. https://www.nytimes.com/2011/03/13/weekinreview/13backthen.html.
Newsweek, "Rector and a Rumpus," July 4, 1960.
Nichol, John Thomas. *Pentecostalism*. New York: Harper & Row, 1966.
Niebuhr, Gustav. "Where Religion Gets a Big Dose of Shopping-Mall Culture," The New York Times, April 16, 1995, 2.
Offutt, Stephen. *New Centers of Global Evangelicalism in Latin America and Africa*. New York: Cambridge University Press, 2015.
Oliver, Jeff. *Pentecost to the Present: Book One: Early Prophetic and Spiritual Gifts*. Newberry, Florida: Bridge Logos, 2017.
Oliverio, L. William. *Theological Hermeneutics in the Classical Pentecostal Tradition: A Typological Account*. Leiden, Netherlands: Brill, 2012.
Owens, Robert R. *The Azusa Street Revival its Roots and Its Message*. Longwood, Florida: Xulon, 2005.
Packer, J. I. *Keep in Step with the Spirit: Finding Fullness in Our Walk with God*. Grand Rapids, Michigan: Baker, 2005.
Pamphilus. *The Sacred Writings of Eusebius Pamphilus*. Altenmünster, Germany: Jazzybee Verlag, 2012.
Parham, Charles. *A Voice Crying in the Wilderness*. Christian Pentecostal Books, 2012.
———. *The Everlasting Gospel*. Christian Pentecostal Books, 2012.
Parham, Sarah E. *The Life of Charles F. Parham, Founder of the Apostolic Faith Movement*. New York: Garland, 1985.
Parvini, Sarah. "Messages in Tongues Down among Pentecostals." *Akron Beacon Journal*, August 31, 2013. https://www.ohio.com/akron/lifestyle/messages-in-tongues-down-among-pentecostals.
Pew Forum on Religion and Public Life. "Spirit and Power: A10-Country Survey of Pentecostals." Pew Research Center, October 2006. http://www.pewforum.org/2006/10/05/spirit-and-power/.
Poloma, Margaret M. and John C. Green. *The Assemblies of God: Godly Love and the Revitalization of American Pentecostalism*. New York: New York University Press, 2010.
———. *Main Street Mystics: The Toronto Blessing and Reviving Pentecostalism*. Walnut Creek, California: Altamira, 2007.
———. "Toronto Blessing." In *The New International Dictionary of Pentecostal and Charismatic Movements*, edited by Stanley Burgess, and Eduard Van Der Mass, 1149–52. Grand Rapids, Michigan: Zondervan, 2002.

Bibliography

Pugh, Ben. *Bold Faith: A Closer Look at the Five Key Ideas of Charismatic Christianity*. Eugene, Oregon: Wipf and Stock, 2017.

Pullum, Stephen J. *Faith Healers and the Bible: What Scripture Really Says*. Santa Barbara, California: Praeger, 2015.

Purdy, Harlyn G. *A Distinct Twenty-First Century Pentecostal Hermeneutic*. Eugene, Oregon: Wipf and Stock, 2015.

Pyle, Hugh F. *The Truth about Tongues and the Charismatic Movement*. Murfreesboro, Tennessee: Sword of the Lord, 1976.

Rabey, Steve. "Brownsville Revival Rolls Onward." *Christianity Today*, February 1998. https://www.christianitytoday.com/ct/1998/february9/8t2080.html.

Robeck, Cecil M. Jr. "Azusa Street: 100 Years Later." Springfield, Missouri: *The General Council of the Assemblies of God*. http://enrichmentjournal.ag.org/200602/200602_026_Azusa.cfm.

———. *The Azusa Street Mission and Revival: The Birth of the Global Pentecostal Movement*. Nashville, Tennessee: Thomas Nelson, 2006.

———. "The Azusa Street Revival." In *The New International Dictionary of Pentecostal and Charismatic Movements*, edited by Stanley Burgess, and Eduard van der Mass, 344–50. Grand Rapids, Michigan: Zondervan, 2002.

———. "Seymour, William Joseph," In *The New International Dictionary of Pentecostal and Charismatic Movements*, edited by Stanley Burgess, and Eduard van der Mass, 1053–1058. Grand Rapids, Michigan: Zondervan.

Roberts, Samuel K. *African American Christian Ethics*. Eugene, Oregon: Wipf and Stock, 2001.

Robinson, J. *Divine Healing: The Years of Expansion, 1906–1930: Theological Variation in the Transatlantic World*. Eugene, Oregon: Wipf and Stock, 2014.

Russell, Henry. "The Gold Rush." In *Mexico and the United States*, edited by Stacy Lee, 367–68. New York: Marshall Cavendish, 2002.

Sanders, Rufus, G. W. *William Joseph Seymour: 1870–1922*. Sandusky, Ohio: Xulon, 2003.

Schaff, Philip. *History of the Christian Church*. Electronic Edition STEP Files. Findex.com, 1999.

Schmitt, Charles. *Floods upon the Dry Ground*. Shippensburg: Destiny Image, 1999.

Scott, C. A. Anderson. "What Happened at Pentecost?" In *The Spirit: The Relation of Man and God Considered from the Standpoint of Philosophy, Psychology and Art*, edited by B. H. Streeter, 117–59. London: Macmillan, 1935.

Seymour, William. *Apostolic Faith*. 1 (September 1906) 1.

———. "Pentecostal Baptism Restored." *Apostolic Faith*, 1 (October 1906) 2.

Shapiro, Stephen and Phillip Barnard. *Pentecostal Modernism. Lovecraft, Los Angeles, and World-Systems Culture*. London: Bloomsbury Academic, 2017.

Smith, Chuck. *Charisma vs. Charismania*. Eugene, Oregon: Harvest House, 1983.

BIBLIOGRAPHY

Smith, David. *Theologies of the 21st Century: Trends in Contemporary Theology*. Eugene, Oregon: Wipf and Stock, 2014.

Smith, Lucy. *Biographical Sketches of Joseph Smith the Prophet: And His Progenitors for Many Generations*. Liverpool, London: S. W. Richards, 1853.

Smith, Warren B. "Holy Laughter or Strong Delusion." Used by Permission for Lighthouse Trails. https://www.lighthousetrailsresearch.com/blog/?p=11935.

Sproul, R. C and Archie Parrish. *The Spirit of Revival: Discovering the Wisdom of Jonathan Edwards*. Wheaton, Illinois: Crossway, 2000.

Stammer, Larry B. "A Spiritual Split: Anaheim-Based Pentecostal Sect Ousts Controversial Group." *Los Angeles Times*, December 10, 1995.

Stanford, Lee. *The Pentecostal Takeover: Why Pentecostals seek Leadership in Non-Pentecostal Churches*. New York: Xulon, 2005.

Stedman, Ray. *Body Life*. Glendale, California: Regal, 1972.

Steinberg, Ted. *Acts of God: The Unnatural History of Natural Disasters in America*. Oxford: Oxford University Press, 2000.

Stephens, Randall J. *The Fire Spreads Holiness and Pentecostalism in the American South*. Cambridge, Massachusetts: Harvard University Press, 2008.

Stjerna, Kirsi, ed. *The Annotated Luther, Volume 2: Word and Faith*. Minneapolis, Minnesota: Fortress, 2015.

St. Louis Post-Dispatch. "New Sect in Kansas Speaks with Strange Tongues." January 1901. https://www.newspapers.com/clip/13018920/st_louis_postdispatch/.

Strand, Paul. "Toronto Blessing: The Greatest Thing That's Happened in the Church in the Last 100 Years." *CBN News*, June 22, 2018. https://www1.cbn.com/cbnnews/world/2018/june/toronto-blessing-the-greatest-thing-thats-happened-in-the-church-in-the-last-100-years.

Sweeden, Joshua R. "Church of the Nazarene." In *Encyclopedia of Christianity in the United States*, edited by George Thomas Kurian, and Mark A. Lamport, 5, 577–79. London: Rowman & Littlefield, 2016.

Sweeney, Douglas. *The American Evangelical Story: A History of the Movement*. Grand Rapids, Michigan: Baker, 2005.

Swincer, David A. *Tongues Volume 1: Confused by the Ecstasy: A Careful Study of the Confusing Element of Ecstasy*. South Australia, Australia: Integrity, 2013.

Synan, Vinson, and Charles R. Fox Jr. *William J. Seymour: Pioneer of the Azusa Street Revival*, edited by Harold J. Chadwick. Alachua, Florida: Bridge-Logos, 2012.

———. *An Eyewitness Remembers the Century of the Holy Spirit*. Grand Rapids, Michigan: Chosen, 2010.

———. *The Holiness-Pentecostal Tradition: Charismatic Movements in the Twentieth Century*. Grand Rapids, Michigan: Eerdmans, 1997.

Bibliography

———. "Parham, Charles Fox." In *Encyclopedia of the Great Plains*, edited by David J. Wishart, 753–54. Lincoln, Nebraska: University of Nebraska Press, 2004.

———. "Pentecostalism." In *The Evangelical Dictionary of Theology*. 2nd ed., edited by Walter A. Elwell, 900–902. Grand Rapids, Michigan: Baker, 2001.

Tennant, Timothy C. *Theology in the Context of World Christianity: How the Global Church is Influencing the Way We Think about and discuss Theology.* Grand Rapids, Michigan: Zondervan, 2007.

Topeka Daily Capital. "A Queer Faith: Strange Actions of the Apostolic Believers." January 6, 1901, 2.

Toronto Life Magazine. "The Best and Worst: A Year in the Life of a City." January 1994.

Torrey, R. A. "The King's Business." July 1913, 360–62. http://scriptoriumdaily.com/the-tongues-movement-is-not-of-god/.

Training Timothys: Equipping the Next Generation of Bible Teachers. https://trainingtimothys.org/library/advanced-theology/.

Turner, Max. *The Holy Spirit and Spiritual Gifts.* Peabody, Massachusetts: Hendrickson, 1998.

Van Biema, David and Jeff Chu. "Does God Want You to Be Rich?" *Time*, September 18, 2006.

Van Dusan, Henry, P. "Third Force in Christendom." *Life Magazine*, 44, 23 (1958) 113–22.

Vondey, Wolfgang. "The Denomination in Classical and Global Pentecostal Ecclesiology: A Historical and Theological Contribution." In *Denominations: Assessing an Ecclesiological Category*, edited by Paul M. Gollins and George Barry Ensign, 100–116. London: T. & T. Clark, 2011.

———. *Pentecostalism a Guide for the Perplexed.* London: T. & T. Clark, 2013.

Wacker, Grant. *Heaven Below: Early Pentecostals and American Culture.* Cambridge, Massachusetts: Harvard University Press, 2001.

Wagner, Peter C. *The Changing Church: How God Is Leading His Church into the Future.* Ventura, California: Regal, 2004.

———. *Wrestling with Alligators, Prophets, and Theologians: Lessons from a Lifetime in the Church: A Memoir.* Ventura, California: Regal, 2010.

Walker, Andrew G. "Thoroughly Modern." In *Notes from a Wayward Son*, edited by Andrew D. Kinsey, 51–73. Eugene, Oregon: Cascade, 2015.

Walker, Laurance R., and Frederick H. Landau, eds. *A Natural History of the Mojave Desert.* Tucson, Arizona: University of Arizona Press, 2018.

Walsh, Sanchez Arlene. *Pentecostals in America.* New York: Columbia University Press, 2018.

Waxman, Sharon. "Filled with the HO-HO-Holy Spirit." *Washington Post*, January, 1996. https://www.washingtonpost.com/archive/lifestyle/1996/01/02/filled-with-ho-ho-holy-spirit/aeb5dced-7018-4e70-90b3-6d407885552f/?noredirect=on.

BIBLIOGRAPHY

Weaver, John. *New Apostolic Reformation: History of a Modern Charismatic Movement*. Jefferson, North Carolina: McFarland, 2016.

Welchel, Tommy, and Michelle Griffith. *True Stories of the Miracles of Azusa Street and Beyond: Re-live One of the Greatest Outpourings*. Shippensburg, Pennsylvania: Destiny Image, 2013.

Whitaker, Robert. "Is California Irreligious?" *Sunset*, 16 (1906) 382–85.

Williams, J. R. "Charismatic Movement." In *The Evangelical Dictionary of Theology*. 2nd ed., edited by Walter A. Elwell, 221–24. Grand Rapids, Michigan: Baker, 2001.

Yamane, David. "Charisma." In *Encyclopedia of Religion and Society*, edited by William H. Swatos Jnr., 78–82. Walnut Creek, California: Altamira, 1998.

Zelizer, Barbie. *About to Die: How News Images Move the Public*. New York: Oxford University Press, 2010.

Ziefle, Joshua R. "The Charismatic Renewal." In *Handbook of Global Contemporary Christianity: Movements, Institutions, and Allegiance*, edited by Stephen Hunt 123–43. Leiden, Netherlands: Brill, 2016.

———. *David du Plessis and the Assemblies of God: The Struggle for the Soul of a Movement: Global Pentecostal and Charismatic Studies*. Leiden, Netherlands: Brill, 2013.

Zoll, Rachel. "Televangelists Escape Penalty in Senate Inquiry." *NBC News*, July 2011. http://www.nbcnews.com/id/40960871/ns/politics-capitol_hill/t/televangelists-escape-penalty-senate-inquiry/.

Index

ABC Network, in the Name of God broadcast, 52
Acts book of,
   modern-day repetition of, 5, 13, 25, 95, 98, 128
   new religion based on, 47
   identification with the early church, 98
   seeking proof text from, 5
   the fire came down just like, 13
African-American, 4, 9, 26, 113
America, 11, 19, 37, 44, 86
   best-known Pentecostal in, 134
   the golden dream resurfaced in, 37
   most Christians live in the least wealthy states, 77
   turning Charismatic? 44
   modern Pentecostalism begins in, ix. *See also* the United States
American Religious Identification Survey (ARIS), 77
Anaheim Vineyard Church, 53
Anderson,
   Alan, 100
   Azusa Street veteran, 14, 15
Anglican, 56
apocalyptic fervor,
   as a driving force in Pentecostalism, 30, 110
   imbibing of, 31

Apostle John the, 100
Apostle Paul the, 80, 104, 122
Apostles, the,
   contrary to, 67
   ceased with, 92
   "distinctive tongues" of, 103
   just like, 25, 101
   the same experience as, 62
   the way of, 96
Apostolic Faith Assemblies, 7
Apostolic Faith magazine,
   bizarre disclaimer of, 29
   the mailing lists disappear, 109
Apostolic Faith,
   Mission, 7, 96, 117
   Movement, 111, 130
Ark of the Covenant, 133
Armstrong, John, 60, 63
Associated Press, 89
Association of Vineyard Churches, 51, 54
Augustine, Saint, 102, 104
Azusa Street Mission, the,
   antagonists of, 118–19
   boosters of, 10
   the central myth of, 12
   and comparisons with Jesus's birthplace of a stable, 12, 33
   like the day of Pentecost revisited, 98
   demolished, 136

Index

Azusa Street Mission, the, *(continued)*
    doctrinal difficulties develop within, 111
    an enigmatic figure emerges at, 111
    flames of fire at, 15
    as a focal point of interest, 26
    growth of after the earthquake, 56
    interracial harmony disrupted at, 116
    the multicultural appeal of, 26
    Pentecostals trace their lineage from, 17, 35
    personal difficulties develop, 108, 115
    pulpit hijacked at, 112
    as the sole point of Pentecostal origin, 11
    strange "glow" at, 13
    a strange smoke-like substance appears at, 14
    as a turning point in Christian history, 24
    the world rushes in, 21, 37

Back to Pentecost, 5, 94, 97, 98, 105
Baptism of the Holy Spirit,
    modern Christians can receive the, 25
    the controversial subject of, 9
    dogmatic insistence on, 84, 116
    empty of any real meaning, 97
    the first person to receive, 4
    not widely accepted, 90
    Parham's view on the, 82–84
    a new version of teaching of, 9
    similar to the Apostles, 25
    speaking in other tongues indicates the, 90
    taking middle-ground on, 93–94
    teaching a distorted view of, 94
    varying opinions of, 94
Baptist. *See* Southern Baptist
Barbare, Donald R., 77
Barfoot, Chas H., 110, 135
Barna Group, 44
Barret, David B., 76
Bartleman, Frank,
    forsakes Seymour, 114, 117
    and earthquake, 26–28
    first chronicler of the Pentecostal movement, 11
    and Pentecostalism, 11
    succumbs to the "oneness" teaching, 115
Bennett, Dennis J., 5, 40–41, 51
Benton, Reverend, Joseph Augustine, 37
Bethel Bible College, 128
Bible, the,
    blunting the blessing of, 64
    twisting verses of, 66
    the gulf between current practices and, 48
    inerrancy of, 49
    major battle for, 61
    mythical understanding of, 88
    Pentecostals read and value, 49
Bible School,
    Seymour attends Knapp's, 31
    in Topeka, Kansas, 3
biblical,
    days, 16, 98
    evidence, 25, 85
    foundation, lack of, 62
    uncertainty, 3
Blumhofer, Edith, 108
Bonnie Bray Street, 10, 13
Borlase, Craig, 114
Bosworth, Fred Francis, 91
Brands, H.W., 37
Bredeson, Harold, 40
Bresee, Phineas F., 124–25
Brownsville, AG Church. *See* Pensacola

Index

Brownsville Revival rolls onward, 72
Bruner, Frederick Dale, 38, 70
Burning Bush Association, 32

Calvary Chapel, 50–51
Calvin, John, x, 103–4
Campolo, Tony, 94
Canada, 22
Cane Ridge Revival, compared with Toronto and Brownsville, 75
Carney, Julie, 15
Carson, D. A., vii
catch the fire, 66, 81
Catch the Fire Toronto, 54
Catholicism, 39, 44
Chan, Simon, 59
Charisma magazine, 43, 73–74
California,
 Anaheim, 53
 "casual style" of, 49
 as the Charismatic Cradle, 6, 33–38, 51
 dreamers, 36
 electrifies the world, 37
 first Congregational Church in, 37
 Golden State of, 20–21, 35
 irreligious? 36–37
 as a land of pilgrimage, 37
 movie capital vs. charismatic capital, 36
 Yorba Linda, 50
California gold rush,
 and the "God Rush" to Azusa Street, 22, 37
 news spreading around the world about, 19
 separating fool's gold from the real, 23
Charismatic Movement,
 looking into the abyss of the, 59
 and the preoccupation with experience, 48

Charismatic Renewal,
 beginning of the, 5, 39–40
 the decline of, 41–43
 the end of the, 43, 58
 the phrase coined, 40
 the second wave of the, 5, 39, 50
 the spread of the, 40
Charismatic Renewal within mainline churches,
 inclusive trend of the, 38
 liberal stance of, 42
 loses members, 43
 Pentecostal ideas spread into, 3
 rates of growth within the, 42
 "subtle inroads" into, 38
Chesnut, Andrew, 26
Christerson, Brad, 46
Christian perfection, 112
Christianity Today, 52 53, 62, 72, 79, 89
Christians,
 "elite band" of, 131
 evangelical, 44, 61
 living below the poverty line, 76
Chrysostom, John, on cessation of tongues, 102–4
Church fathers on cessation of tongues, 100
Cincinnati, Ohio, 30
Cold War, 39
Coloma Creek. *See* Gold rush
color line, 115
Conkin, Paul K., 127
Cottrell, Jack, 65
Cox, Harvey, 75, 90
cradle,
 of the Charismatic Movement, 35–36
 of Christianity, 35
 of the Pentecostal movement, 10, 25–26
 of power, 50
 of revivals, 35

Index

Crawford, Florence,
  disagrees with Seymour's marriage, 108
  forms an independent work in Portland, Oregon, 109–11
Creech, Joseph, 10

Dager, Albert James, 61
dental amalgam transformation. *See* gold fillings
devotional tongues. *See* speaking in tongues
discernment,
  genuine from the fake, 23
  biblical, x
doctrine,
  distorted, 94
  flaky, 43
  strange, 49
  of tongues questioned, 91–92
drunk in the spirit phenomena, 56
Durham, William,
  divides the Pentecostal movement, 113
  and the Finished Work teaching, 112, 114
  as interim pastor at Azusa Street, 111–12
  his unpleasant confrontation with Seymour, 113

early church,
  actions and experiences of the, 48
  returning to the days of the, 96–98, 117
earthquake. *See* San Francisco earthquake
Economist magazine, 1, 36
ecstatic,
  experiences, 43, 70
  phenomena, 61, 70–71
  speech, 82
  utterances, 141
Eden, Garden of,
  and Parham's theory as the lost city of Atlantis, 132
  and Parham's two separate species of humanity, 131
Eddie, Mary-Baker, 80
Eifler, Mark A., 22
Episcopalians, 5, 39–40
Espinosa, Gaston, 112, 116, 132
Eternity Magazine, 40
Eusebius, 70
Evangelical Dictionary of Theology, 34
Evening Light Saints Movement, 67
experiences,
  extra-biblical, 58, 69
  must be Bible-based, 140
eyewitness accounts. *See* Azusa Street

faith healers, 38, 76
falling,
  under the power, 56
  at Azusa Street, 65–66, 72
  in biblical times, 67
  the position of the AG on, 69
  in pagan cultures, 68
  into trances, 53, 71. *See also* slain in the Spirit
Father's Day, 1995. *See* Pensacola AG Church,
Fenwick, Peter, 61–62
Finished Work teaching, 112, 114
Fitzpatrick, Truman, 77
Flory, Richard, 46
Flynn, Leslie B., 104
folklore. *See* mythology
fool's gold, 22–24. *See also* California gold rush
foundation myth. *See* mythology
Freemasonry, Parham's Association with, 130
Fudge, T. A., 115
Fuller Theological Seminary, 6, 45–46, 50

Index

Galmond, Mary, 29
Gardiner, George, 48
Garr, Lillian and Alfred G., 32, 86–88
gifts,
   Episcopalians succumbing to, 80
   the ceasing of the miraculous, 99–104
   charismatic, 44
   prophetic, 100
   served their purpose, 104
Global Financial Crisis (GFC), 76
Godbey, William Baxter,
   arrives at Azusa Street, 112–13, 121–22
   his opinion of Pentecostalism, 122
Goff, James R., 124, 127, 130, 134–35
Golden State. *See* California
gospel,
   another, 112
   displacing of the, 60–61
   full, 128
   guardians of the, 100, 105
   partial, 95
   selling out of the, 53
   token knowledge of the, 65
   toning down of the, 60
Govan, Chloe, 57
Grace,
   second work of, 112
   third work of, 113, 115
Grady, Lee, 73–74
Graham, Billy, 79, 93–94

Hanegraaff, Hank, 52, 65
Hayford, Jack, 11, 85
healing,
   advanced courses offered in, 63
   after-class sessions, 46
Health and Wealth gospel. *See* prosperity gospel
Hoekema, Anthony, 94

Holiness Movement, 122
Hinduism, 68
Hinn, Costi, 46
Holliday, J. S., 21
Holy Jumpers, 32
Holy Spirit,
   filled with the, 13, 44, 94
   not all phenomena from the, 23–24
   in every believer, viii
   Holy Trinity Church Brompton, 98
Hollywood, 1, 2, 36
Hunt, Stephen, 58
Hunter, Harold, 13
Hutchins, Julia, 9
hypnotic,
   consciousness, 120
   current, 66
   happenings, 122–24
   controls, 83
   state, 65. *See also* slain in the Spirit
hysteria,
   that is best-forgotten, 52, 54
   and the Third Wave Movement's focus on, 52, 64

Ignited Church. *See* Lakeland AG
initial evidence,
   teaching not widely accepted around the world, 90
   as a door to deception, 84, 124
   as an erroneous belief, 91
   tongues as primary evidence of the, 84
Irenaeus, Saint, 100, 102
Ironside, Harry A., 125

Jacobson, Douglas, 11, 108
Jerusalem, 29, 134
Jesus Christ, x, xi, 12, 33, 63, 91, 105
Johns, Kenneth D., 70–71
Johnson Todd. M., 76

157

Index

jungle chorus, 57
Jurgensmeier Kurt, xi, 42, 63

Kansas City, Missouri, 41
Kennedy, J.F., 39
Knapp, Martin Wells, 31
Kostlevy, William, 32
Ku Klux Klan, Parham's support of, 130
Kundalini. *See* slain in the Spirit,
Kuyper, Abraham, 97

Lakeland AG Church, 51, 55, 62, 72–75
 "didn't ring true," 74
 ignited, 73
 laughter in, 73
 poison traveled from, 74
 "run for the exits," 75
languages,
 foreign human, ix
 gibberish, 40
 native, 84, 86, 88, 100–101
 unlearned human, 9
 unintelligible prayer language, 83, 86
 unusual, 4
 various, 16. *See also* speaking in tongues
Larkin, Clarence, 65
Latourette, Kenneth, ix,
laughing, 68, 72
 excessive, 52
 for the Lord, 52
 and not deep repentance, 75
 rolling around and, 61
 uncontrollably during the services, 55
Lausanne Movement, 78–80
Liardon, Roberts, 99
Life Magazine, 2, 38
Lifeway Research,
 Tongues Survey Fuels Baptist Debate, 92

timing of the survey questioned, 92–93
Los Angeles,
 Azusa Street, xiii, 10
 at a crossroad, 24
 as the cradle of Pentecostal tradition, 25
 as a cradle of revivals, 35
 the demise of the Pentecostal base in, 109
 Durham's arrival in, 113
 earthquake aftershocks felt in, 27
 is electrified, 121
 the first wave of the Pentecostal movement in, 5
 a focal point of interest in, 26
 How Pentecost Came to, 11
 as a melting pot, 25
 new religious phenomena beginning in, 21
 prophecies of earthquakes coming to, 29
 a new wave of Pentecost comes to, 95
 Parham's hurried journey to, 123
 population growth of, 20
 the second wave of the Pentecostal movement in, 40
 Seymour travels to, 9
 on tiptoe with expectancy, 113
Los Angeles Daily Times, 4, 18, 33, 40, 55, 81
Los Angeles Herald, 20
Luke, the writer of the book of Acts, 47
Lum, Clara, 109–10
Luther, Martin, xi, 102–3, 128
Lutzer, Erwin, 61, 67, 70

MacArthur, John, viii, 6, 8, 12, 23–24, 64, 67, 70, 76, 86, 88, 130, 132

Index

mainline churches, 3, 38. *See also* Charismatic Renewal within
Marshall, James, 19, 22
media reports,
   abuzz with strange Pentecostal-type phenomena, 52
   and the debut of Pentecostalism, 4
   dub "the Toronto Blessing," 56
   on the "prosperity gospel," 76, 79–80
   on the San Francisco earthquake, 19
   about the Third Wave Movement, 53
megachurches, 86
mental gymnastics, 91
Metropolitan Church Association (MCA), 32
miracle healing. *See* the Third Wave movement
miracles
   begin to fade, 62
   "character" rather than "charismatic," 63
   emphasis upon, 39, 60
   as an everyday occurrence, 5
   minus the, 119
   modern churches and, 103
   as a normative experience, 37
   purported, 65
Mittelstadt, Martin William, 87
Mohler, Albert, 80
Montanism,
   Montanus, leader of, 70
   similarities to Pentecostalism, 70
Montier, Gerald and Carolyn, 117
Moody, D.L., 119
Moody Bible Church, 125
Moody, David, 100
Moore, David, 11, 85
Moore, Jenny, 15, 108, 110
Morgan, G. Campbell, 125
Mormons, 10, 105

mystical miracle movement, 46
mythological occurrences,
   and folklore, 11–16, 88
   as a foundation myth, 10
   and the Pentecostal myth of origin, 10, 135

Neo-Pentecostalism. *See also* Charismatic Renewal
   assumes the name of the Charismatic Renewal, 38, 40
   permeates mainline churches, 39
new experiences, search for, 59
new generational church, 44
New Pentecost, the, 38
New York Times, 7, 13, 14, 33, 119
Newman, Larry Vern, 100, 105
Newsweek, magazine, 40
Nichol, John Thomas, 102, 116

Oakland Baptist Church, 36
Oneness Movement, 115
Owens, Robert R., 129
Ozman, Agnes, 4

Pacific Faith Movement, Seymour bishop of, 117
Packer, James Innell, 47
Parham, Charles,
   character assessment of, 8, 120, 128
   controversial views of, 130–32
   his death in 1929, 135
   discovers tongues phenomena, 4
   his ill-fated venture, 133–34
   important religious pioneer, 135
   last trip abroad, 135
   legacy of, 135
   an unwelcome guest at Azusa Street, 123
Parham, Sarah, 9, 122, 130
Parrish, Archie, 23

Index

Pastoral Renewal magazine, 45
Pearson International Airport, 54
Pensacola AG Church, 51, 59, 72–73
Pentecostal Church of the Nazarene, 12
Pentecostal Evangel, 4
Pentecostalism,
  the epicenter of, 7, 11, 108
  early pioneers of, 127
  the formulator of, 120, 126, 129
  a new constellation of, 38
  Parham's contribution to, 129
  roots of, viii, xiii, 8, 50, 127–28
Pentecostal movement, the
  attractions of, 23
  as a beacon of equality and hope, 26
  eyewitnesses accounts of, xiv, 10, 12–13, 16, 118
  and growth of, 2, 25
  the global phenomenon of, 2, 6, 107
  and the gold rush, 23
  "haves" and "have-nots" aspects of, vii
  and the high regard held for the, 12
  "hopelessly divided," 115
  identity at risk, 90
  and key "triggers of," 20
  leaps 2,000 years of church history, 5, 96–100
  left divided, 135
  the launching point of, xiii
  nervous "Los Angelinos" rush to join, 26
  oneness teaching endemic among, 115
  personalities of, xiv, 77
  as out-of-step with Bible teaching, 121
  as out-of-step with Parham's teaching, 83
  and San Francisco earthquake, 53
  sincere in its approach to biblical truth, 126
  in "total disarray," 115
Pentecostals,
  classic, number of, 50
  and the decline of tongues, 90
  origins of, 7, 11, 127, 135, 137
Pew Research Center, 78, 89–90
Poloma Margaret, 35, 48–49, 64, 92
Polycarp, bishop of Smyrna, 100
power,
  baptismal, 83
  of the cross, 114
  evangelism, 64.
  jolted with spiritual, 68
  the old cradle of, 114
  witnessed the, 72
  the quest for more, 64
prayer language. *See* languages
prayer meeting, tongues of fire swirling, 13, 33
prosperity gospel,
  critique of, 79–80
  general appeal or lack thereof, 78
  making inroads into Pentecostalism, 78
  name-it-and-claim aspect of, 52, 75
  a new wave surging through the church, 76
  the popularity of, 79
  testing its hypotheses, 77
Protestantism, 39
Pugh, Ben, 45
Purdy, Harlyn Graydon, 128
Pullum, Stephen J., 67

racism, 111, 116–17
radical,
  fly-by-night mystical group, 70
  network, 32

theories endorsed by Parham, 31, 133
restoration of miracles. *See* Third Wave Movement
Robeck, Cecil M. Jr., 11, 13, 23, 71
rumors,
 of an attempted takeover at Azusa Street, 114
 of "tongues of fire," 33
 of a "tremendous party going on," 57
"routinization of charisma," 59

San Francisco, 1, 21
San Francisco earthquake, 1, 18, 36
 "domino" effect of the, 26
 did God send the? 27
 will not come on Sunday, 29
Schaff, Philip, ix
Scripture,
 using to justify strange phenomena, 66
 the gold standard of, 22. *See also* Bible
Seymour, William,
 the acknowledged leader of Pentecostalism, 8
 his apocalyptic outlook, 30
 in Cincinnati, Ohio, 30
 clashes with Parham over the tongues issue, 84
 and the Durham debacle, 111–15
 on earthquake as the great tribulation, 29
 and God's Bible School, 31
 key staff parted ways with, 108
 in Los Angeles, 9–10
 his marriage, 15, 108, 110
 and mailing list disappearance, 109–10
 as "part of the radical network," 32
 playing in the thick cloud, 14–15
 public image, 8, 128
 rejects Finished Work teaching, 112
 his stance on speaking in tongues shifts, 84, 85
 as a student, 9
 views on marriage, 110–11
 his successor as a person of color, 117
Shakespeare, William, 22
Shaktipat. *See* slain in the Spirit
signs and wonders, 32, 46, 49, 53, 61
singing in tongues, 16
slain in the Spirit, 64–70
 absent in the scriptures, 67
 another sort of consciousness, 64
 the biblical warrant for, 66
 as "carpet time," 57, 66
 courtesy fall, 69
 kundalini aspect of, 68
 Parham on, 65–66
Smith, Chuck, 48
Smith, Joseph, 105
Smith, Lucy, 105
something more, search for, 59
something new 45, 59, 62, 69–70
 the continual search for, 59
 looking for, 45
sound biblical teaching,
 lack of, 48
 is often thrown aside, 70
Southern Baptists, the,
 changing views on tongues speaking, 93
 on a private prayer language, 92
Speaking in tongues,
 Assemblies of God and, 90–92
 ceased with the apostles, 99–104

Index

Speaking in tongues, *(continued)*
  Corinthian Church and, 71, 101, 104
  decreasing popularity of, 89–90
  the decline is "totally inaccurate," 89
  distinctive vs. devotional, 103
  the early church and, 100, 102
  the first person to receive, 4
  heavenly vs. real language, 83
  literal foreign language, 86
  Mormons example of, 105
  Parham's view of, 83
  private use of, 101
  as a restored prayer language, 103
  Seymour's stance on, 85
  the stigma attached to, 90
  as a tool for evangelism, 83
Sproul, R.C., 23
Stanford, Lee, 105
Stedman, Ray, 101
St Mark's Church. *See* Episcopalians
St Louis Post-Dispatch, 4
Sunset magazine, 36
Sweeney, Douglas, 38
Synan, Vinson, 25, 62, 74, 87, 125

Telegraph, London, 56
televangelists,
  media reports focus on, 76
  Senate inquiry of, 77–78
Third Force in Christendom. *See* Charismatic Movement
Third Wave Movement, the,
  blunts the force of the gospel, 64
  controversial aspects of, 54
  development of, 45
  downplays the tongues phenomena, 49
  growth of, 7, 49–50
  the paradigm shift of, 65
  phenomena associated with, 52
  and the restoration of miracles, 49
  unquestionable and uncritical acceptance of, 62
Time magazine, 40, 78
toggling tongues, 86
Tongues. *See* Speaking in tongues
Topeka Daily Capital newspaper, 4
Topeka, Kansas, xiii, 3–4, 8, 128
Toronto Airport Christian Fellowship, 54
Toronto Airport Vineyard Church, 54
Toronto Blessing, the,
  arrival on British shores, 56–58
  as the best party in the whole universe, 60
  captures the world's attention, 54
  controversial aspects of, 54
  finally "blown out," 58
  finally worn off? 59
  gold fillings miraculously appearing, 66
  lasting benefits of, 54
  misgivings about, 61
  never waned, 55
  next waves to appear after the, 72
  as an offshoot of the Vineyard movement, 53
  or not? 53
  origins of the British derivative, 56–57
  reached a "new low," 63
  the spiritual split, 50, 54–55
  as Toronto's top tourist attraction, 55
  "trivial pursuit" after, 63
  as yesterday's news, 58
Toronto Life magazine, 56
Torrey, R.A.,
  and his assessment of Pentecostalism

INDEX

his stream of teaching as a basis
for Pentecostalism, 119
his tirade, 120
Trask, Thomas, 72
Trinity mention of, 115
Turner, Max, x
The United Kingdom, 56–58
The United States,
largest Protestant denomination in, 92
percentage of Pentecostals in, xiii, 44

Van Nuys, California, 5, 39
Vineyard Movement. See Wimber, John
Vondey, Wolfgang, 6

Wacker, Grant, 88
Wagner, Peter C., 45–46
Walker, Andrew G., 58, 59

Washington Post, 79, 93
Welchel, Tommy, 14
Wesley, John, 86, 128
Whitaker, Robert, 36–37
Wimber, John,
his association with the Toronto Blessing, 51
at Fuller Theological Seminary, 45
launches Vineyard Movement, 50
splits with Vineyard associated church, 51, 55
Wood, Anthony, 46
Word of Faith Movement. See Prosperity Gospel,
Word of God. See Bible

Yerba Buena. See California

Ziefle, Joshua, R., 12

163

www.ingramcontent.com/pod-product-compliance
Lightning Source LLC
Chambersburg PA
CBHW062002180426
43198CB00036B/2140